Pirates and Their Flags

The Jolly Roger and the Golden Age of Piracy

Matthew Leigh Embleton

Copyright ©2020 Matthew Leigh Embleton. All rights reserved.

Pirates and Their Flags

1. Origins 1
   The Origin of the term Pirate 1
   The Privateer 1
   The Corsair 1
   The Buccaneer 1
   Filibusters and Freebooters 1
   The Early Years 2
2. The Red Flag and the Buccaneers 4
   Alexandre Exquemelin 4
   François Grogniet 5
   François 'Jambe de Bois' Le Clerc 5
   François l'Olonnais 5
   Jacques Raveneau de Lussan 7
   L'Anonyme de Carpentras 7
   Michel de Grammont 7
   Michel 'Le Basque' Etchegorria 7
   Pierre 'Le Grand' 8
   Pierre le Picard 8
   Claes Gerritszoon Compaen 9
   Edmund Cooke 10
3. The Black Flag and the Pirate Round 12
   The Black Flag 12
   The Skull & Crossbones 13
   The Jolly Roger or Old Roger 14
   The Pirate Round 16
   Emanuel Wynn 17
   Henry Every 18
   Thomas Tew 22
4. The High Tide 24
   Bartholomew 'Black Bart' Roberts 25
   Captain Napin 29
   Charles Harris 30
   Christopher Condent 32
   Christopher Moody and William Moody 33
   Edward 'Blackbeard' Teach 36
   Edward England 38
   Edward 'Ned' Low 40
   Francis Spriggs 43
   George Lowther 44
   Jean Thomas Dulaien 45
   Jeremiah Cocklyn 48
   John 'Calico Jack' Rackham 49
   Anne Bonny 50
   Mary Read 50
   John Phillips 51
   Olivier 'La Buse' Levasseur 53
   Richard Worley 56
   Samuel 'Black Sam' Bellamy 58
   Stede Bonnet 60
   Thomas Nichols 62

Walter Kennedy	65
5. The Later Years	67
Anonymous	68
Ching Shih	69
The Florida Straits Pirates	72

Cover: A selection of pirate flags

All flag images in this book, including its cover, are sourced from Wikipedia Creative Commons and are in the public domain.

Acknowledgments

I have long been fascinated by history, and I am very grateful to the special people in my life who have supported and encouraged me in my work. Thank you for believing in me. You know who you are.

Thanks to Aideen Gannon and Karwing Tang for their input regarding the flag of Ching Shih.

Introduction

I admit it. I am obsessed with pirate flags. I find them fascinating, the different designs and symbols, how they evolved, and how some of them have become widely and instantly recognisable in many ways. I have a wardrobe full of t-shirts with different pirate flags printed on them. If like me you find pirate flags interesting and would like to know more about them, this is the book for you!

For as long as there have been seafarers transporting valuable goods by sea, there have also been pirates. The Golden Age of Piracy began in the 1650s with so-called 'buccaneers' attacking colonies and shipping in the Caribbean and eastern Pacific. This was followed in the 1690s by attacks along the East India Company trade routes in the Indian Ocean and the Red Sea. Finally, when the War of Spanish Succession ended in 1715, thousands of experienced seamen left military duty and turned to piracy, just as the Atlantic shipping trade was beginning to boom.

From the portrayal of piracy in popular culture, whether based on fact, fiction, romanticised legend, from evil antagonist to anti-hero to loveable rogue, or a combination of all of these, we have inherited a set of images conjured up in the mind's eye when we think of pirates, the wooden leg, the parrot perched on the shoulder, the eyepatch, and the stylised accent from the south west of England popularised by Robert Newton in the 1950 film adaptation of 'Treasure Island'.

The Jolly Roger or the Skull & Crossbones is another image that comes to immediately to mind when thinking of pirates, a powerful image of mortality whose origins can be traced as far back as the Late Middle Ages. The use of these symbols by pirates on their flags was designed to strike fear into their prey and encourage them to surrender without a fight. They were also a form of brand identity that would carry with them and reinforce the power of the reputation that preceded them. This book examines the origins, history, and evolution of these flags and their common themes and variations.

Note: Because of the high amount of black ink required to print this book, and to avoid the ink running and pages sticking together, it has been necessary to print this book on premium quality colour paper, which does make it a little bit more expensive. Your understanding is very much appreciated.

1. Origins

The Origin of the term Pirate

The word pirate comes from the Greek *'peira'* (an attempt), *'peirein'* (to attempt to attack), which became *'peirates'*, and was then Latinised as *'pirata'* before entering Middle English as 'pirate' around the year 1300. Spelling was not yet standardised at this time, so alternative spellings exist such as *'pirrot'*, *'pyrat'*, and *'pyrate'*.

The Privateer

A privateer was a private person or vessel that was licensed by their government to attack foreign vessels of countries they were at war with. This license was called a 'letter of marque and reprisal' or 'letter of marque' and is known to have dated back to the Middle Ages. It proved to be an effective way of expanding a nation's naval capability against an enemy or threat.

Privateering was very much viewed as an honourable profession, carried out by brave patriotic adventurers boldly exploring the high seas and the new world in search for enemy vessels as a prize of fortune and glory.

The Corsair

A corsair was a kind of privateer originally known for having operated in the Mediterranean Sea before the increase in activity in the Caribbean where the term also applied. The French for letter of marquee was *'lettre de marquee'* or *'lettre de course'*, hence the term 'corsair'.

The Buccaneer

A buccaneer was a privateer settled and based in the uninhabited areas of the north of Hispaniola (Haiti and the Dominican Republic) and later Tortuga (a small island to the north Haiti) from around 1625 onwards. They were made up of French and English Protestants, and later Dutch. Originally they lived as hunters, but gradually over time they increasingly turned to piracy. From the position of Hispaniola and Tortuga they were able to launch frequent attacks on Spanish ships containing valuable cargo on their return journey to Spain.

They hunted wild boar and cattle and smoked the meat over a slow fire using a small wooden frame called a *'boucan'* (French) or *'bucanero'* (Spanish), a method learned from the Taino and Carib peoples who called it a *'buccan'*. The French word describing such a person was *'boucanier'*, which later became anglicised as 'buccaneer'. The activity of raiding Spanish ships from this position became known as 'buccaneering'.

Filibusters and Freebooters

Filibuster was a term originally used by the Spanish to describe persons raiding Spanish colonies and ships in the West Indies. Both 'filibuster' and 'freebooter', originate from the Dutch word *'vrijbuiter'* (*vrij* = free + *buit* = booty + *er* = agent), which translates directly into English as 'freebooter', but entered Spanish as *'filibustero'* and French as *'flibustier'*.

The Flag of the Spanish Empire

The Early Years

During the 15th century there was an increase in exploration by sea in search of new lands and trading routes. This was intended to break the hold that the Republic of Venice had on the spice trade from the east which was an important part of the economy that had made Venice wealthy and powerful.

Portuguese explorers sailed the North Atlantic and discovered the archipelagos of Madeira in 1419 and Azores in 1427. Exploration continued further south along the west coast of Africa eventually reaching its south-western tip discovering a new sea route to India. Portugal became wealthier as a result of this increase in trade.

In 1492 Christopher Columbus, sponsored by Ferdinand and Isabella of Spain, set sail west in the opposite direction hoping to find an alternative route to India, and so when he arrived in the Caribbean Islands, he believed that he had found India (The Norse exploration of the American continent 500 years earlier as described in the Vínland Sagas was perhaps not widely known at this time) and so began the Spanish colonisation of the Americas. The Caribbean Islands became the Spanish West Indies and the mainland was referred to as The Spanish Main.

To settle the rivalry between Portugal and Spain over the discovery and control of new lands, the Treaty of Tordesillas was ratified by Pope Julius II in 1494. The treaty described a dividing line or 'meridian' that was 370 leagues west of the Cape Verde Islands off the west coast of Africa. Lands to the East of the line would belong to Portugal, and lands to the West of the line would belong to Spain. The treaty left out all of the other European powers, and so it was largely ignored by other European countries, particularly those that became Protestant after the Protestant Reformation challenged the authority of the pope.

In 1519 Ferdinand Magellan organised and set off on an expedition to the East Indies and the so called 'Spice Islands' (Maluku Islands, Indonesia). He successfully navigated from the Atlantic to the Pacific Ocean, but he did not survive the expedition himself being killed in the Philippines.

The remaining survivors (18 or 19 from the original 270 men) returned to Spain in 1522, completing the first circumnavigation of the globe. The navigable route that Magellan found between Chile and the island of Tierra del Fuego he called *Estrecho de Todos los Santos* or 'Strait of All Saints'.

The King of Spain Charles V who had financed the expedition renamed it to the Strait of Magellan to honour him.

The first person to personally circumnavigate the globe was Francis Drake from 1577 to 1580. Licensed by Queen Elizabeth I as a 'voyage of discovery', it was in fact a privateer raiding voyage marking the beginning of England's challenge to Spain's global domination. Francis Drake became known to the Spanish as *El Draque* meaning 'the dragon', and thus they branded him as a pirate.

Massive amounts of wealth in the form of gold, silver, gemstones, spices, hardwoods, and animal skins were shipped back to Spain, and while these Spanish ships were on their return journey fully laden with valuable goods, navigating their way through the 'Windward Passage' (the strait between Cuba and Hispaniola in the Caribbean Sea), they not only faced the threat of hurricanes, they also increasingly became a target for buccaneers who were mostly made up of French and English Protestants.

The Thirty Years War started in 1618 as a conflict between Catholic and Protestant states of Central Europe. The war devastated Protestant communities in France and as a result Protestant French privateers were issued with letters of marque to raid Catholic French and Spanish shipping and territories.

Buccaneers had begun to establish themselves in the uninhabited parts of the north of Hispaniola from about 1625 onwards. They lived off the land and hunted with large calibre hunting muskets which were around 5.5 feet in length (approximately 1.67 metres). They became very effective marksmen, a skill which they began to use to devastating effect against the Spanish.

The Spanish attempted to wipe out both the buccaneers in Hispaniola and the animals they depended on for food, but this had the effect of driving them to nearby Tortuga which proved easier for the buccaneers to defend. This also limited the resources they had access to for survival, which resulted in an increase in raiding activity.

They were soon joined by many more French, English, and later Dutch adventurers and privateers, and with the encouragement of Spain's rivals they increased in strength and number and expanded from attacking Spanish galleons to also sailing further around the Spanish Main sacking cities.

Once the English had captured Jamaica from Spain in 1655, the early English governors of Jamaica issued many more letters of marque to privateers and attacks increased rapidly.

The buccaneers coordinated their activities and efforts and formed a loose coalition or syndicate known as the Brethren of the Coast, who organised themselves by codes of conduct, later referred to as a pirate code, pirate articles, or articles of agreement, this discipline and organisation would have made them an even more formidable enemy.

These pirate codes included rules for discipline of conduct, how the stolen goods would be divided up among the crew, and even rates of compensation for injuries.

2. The Red Flag and the Buccaneers

The Red Flag

When approaching a target vessel, the buccaneers raised the red flag along with the flag of their own nation. It was designed to convey the message that the attackers would not consider themselves bound by the usual rules of engagement, i.e. sparing the lives of those they defeated if resistance was met, but if they were met with immediate surrender however, then the attacking ship would usually give quarter.

The flag was known by the buccaneers as '*joli rouge*' (pretty red) which became 'jolly roger' in English, a term which by association came to refer to pirate flags in general, regardless of their colour or design.

Alexandre Exquemelin

Alexandre Exquemelin (Esquemeling, Exqumeling, or Oexmelin) was born around 1645 and was French, Dutch, or Flemish.

He joined the Dutch East India Company in 1657 as a cabin boy until the ship he was on wrecked on the west coast of Australia. The crew of the ship made their way to Java where Alexandre apprenticed as a barber-surgeon, returning to Holland in 1665.

He joined the French West India Company a year later, which soon afterwards had its grant revoked and was dissolved soon after he arrived in Tortuga. He was then forced into indentured servitude, a kind of labour contract often in return for being transported to a new place. He was rescued from servitude by a physician who healed him and trained him for a year before he sought employment with buccaneers and privateers such as Henry Morgan.

He is known for writing one of the most important books about the buccaneering period entitled 'De Americaensche Zee-Roovers' (The Buccaneers of America) published in English in 1684.

François Grogniet

François and fellow *flibustier* Jean L'Escayer teamed up with English buccaneers Francis Townley, Edward Davis, Charles Swan, and Peter Harris, and were later joined by Marthurin Desmaretsz and Pierre le Picard. They attacked the Spanish treasure fleet and had the advantage of more ships, but were outgunned by the Spanish galleons.

Grogniet's ship was not fitted out with cannons and so his 308-man ship kept its distance and avoided engaging the Spanish. When the attack was called off, Grogniet was blamed in part for the plan's failure and the fleet went their separate ways.

After raiding up the coast to Nicaragua looting towns along the way, Grogniet and his crew were caught by Spanish vessels that attacked and burned their ships. This forced them to march overland towards the Isthmus of Darien before they were rescued by Francis Townley.

They attacked Spanish settlements in Grenada for approximately a month, meeting up with an English force in 1687 to sack Guayaquil in Ecuador. This is where Grogniet received an injury which he finally died from several months later. The remaining forces set sail for the Caribbean Sea.

François 'Jambe de Bois' Le Clerc

François was known as '*Jambe de Bois*' or '*Pata de Palo*' because of his wooden leg, which was perhaps the inspiration for the character Long John Silver in Robert Louis Stephenson's book 'Treasure Island', which popularised the image of a pirate with a wooden leg in popular culture.

In 1553 he attacked the port of Santa Cruz de La Palma in the Canary Islands, looting it and setting it on fire. Next he turned his attention to raiding San Germán in Puerto Rico, after which he then systematically looted all of the ports of Hispaniola and Cuba one by one.

He took over and sacked Santiago de Cuba (the first capital of Cuba) in 1554, and left with 80,000 pesos in treasure. Santiago de Cuba never recovered and the city of Havana became the capital. On his return voyage he plundered Las Palmas on Grand Canary Island and captured a Genoese ship.

They settled the island of St Lucia, using the nearby Pigeon Island to target Spanish treasure galleons. He also attacked a number of settlements along the coast of Panama while waiting for a Spanish fleet carrying gold and silver.

In April 1562 he took part in the rebellion against Catholic rule in his native Normandy alongside Queen Elizabeth I of England's troops by attacking French ships. He asked Queen Elizabeth for a pension, but was not granted one, and instead sailed to the Azores to hunt more Spanish treasure ships, where he died in 1563.

François l'Olonnais

Born around 1630 Jean-David Nau was better known as François l'Olonnais.

After being shipwrecked near Campeche in Mexico, l'Olonnais and his crew were attacked by Spanish soldiers. Almost all of them were killed, and l'Olonnais himself survived by covering himself with blood and hiding among the dead until the Spanish soldiers left.

When he reached Tortuga, he and his crew held a town hostage. A ship was sent by the governor of Havana to kill them, but l'Olonnais captured and beheaded all but one of the crew sent to kill him. The remaining crew member was spared so that he could pass the message to Havana that:

> *"I shall never henceforward give quarter to any Spaniard whatsoever".*

He earned himself the nickname 'Flail of the Spanish' or 'The Bane of Spain'.

In 1666 he joined forces with fellow buccaneer Michel le Basque and while on their way to sack Maracaibo in Venezuela, they came across a Spanish treasure ship, which they captured and found a cargo of cocoa beans, gemstones, and more than 260,000 Spanish dollars (silver coins worth eight Spanish Reales, hence the name 'pieces of eight').

The entrance to Lake Maracaibo was defended by a fortress with sixteen guns and was thought to be impregnable, but they simple attacked it from the landward side which was undefended. They then pillaged the city, demolishing most of the fortifications and taking their cannons. They found however that most of the residents had left the city and hidden their gold.

L'Olonnais and his men tracked down the residents and tortured them until they revealed the locations of their buried valuables, using all manner of brutal and gruesome techniques, slicing off the victim's flesh with a sword, burning them alive, and tying rope around the victim's head and tightening it until their eyes were forced out of their head, to name but a few.

After word had spread of his actions, around seven hundred buccaneers had joined his crew for his next expedition to Honduras. He was again ambushed by Spanish soldiers and again barely survived, capturing two Spaniards and brutally killing one of them by cutting out his heart and biting and gnawing at it while the other Spaniard looked on terrified, and soon told l'Olonnais of a route that would take him to San Pedro.

From there they continued with attacks on Campeche, San Pedro Sula, and Guatemala, and attempted to reach inland cities of Nicaragua by river. He was defeated and once again barely escaped with his life at the hands of the indigenous peoples of the region.

He headed for Cartagena in Colombia but was captured by indigenous people from Darién and killed in a brutal fashion, torn limb from limb and thrown into a fire.

Some might say that it would be a fitting end or a kind of poetic justice catching up with l'Olonnais, someone who had shown similar cruelty to his victims, that he should meet his end in this way.

This level of brutality and sadistic cruelty paints a much darker picture of buccaneers and pirates than the romanticised swash-buckling loveable rogues seen in film and television.

To some buccaneers and pirates, torture and killing was a last resort, a necessary evil which could be called upon to quicken the submission and surrender of their victims. For some however, it was an activity that they appeared to relish.

Jacques Raveneau de Lussan

Born in 1663 in Paris, Jacques embraced a military career at the age of 14. At the age of 17 he headed for Hispaniola in search of fortune, joining the buccaneers under Laurens de Graaf, and then setting out on his own soon after.

After pillaging and sacking El Realejo in Nicaragua, Grenada, and Guayaquil in Ecuador, Jacques and his crew decided to attempt to avoid the Spanish while marching to Nueva Segovia in Nicaragua, accessing the Coco River which leads to the Atlantic Ocean, and then sailing to the Antilles.

After being continually attacked by Spanish troops that vastly outnumbered them, they found a mountain path that led around a narrow pass where the Spanish were entrenched, they were then able to launch a surprise attack from behind giving them the upper hand and victory.

On an English vessel, nearly two months later, Lussan reached Hispaniola and later wrote about his exploits in '*Journal du voyage fait à la mer du Sud avec les flibustiers de l'Amérique*' (Journal of the voyage made to the South Sea with the buccaneers of America).

L'Anonyme de Carpentras

L'Anonyme de Carpentras (The Anonymous of Carpentras) is the name given to an anonymous writer who gave an account of a voyage from Dieppe in 1618, which is preserved in an 88 page manuscript in the Carpentras Library in Southern France.

The account of this voyage is known as 'An account of an unfortunate trip made to the West Indies by Captain Fleury with the description of some islands that one meets there' (*Relation d'un voyage infortuné fait aux Indes occidentales par le capitaine Fleury avec la description de quelques îles qu'on y rencontre*').

They sailed to the Cape Verde Islands, Brazil, Martinique, the Greater Antilles, the coasts of Campeche in Mexico, and as far as Florida before returning to France in 1620. This is the oldest description of a complete trip of a buccaneer, the oldest source describing the indigenous Caribbeans of the Lesser Antilles, and the oldest description of Martinique fifteen years before it was officially colonised by France in 1635.

Michel de Grammont

Born around 1645, Michel de Grammont was forced to leave France after killing a man who was courting his sister. He became a privateer and is known for attacking the Spanish in Venezuela (Maracaibo, Gibraltar, Trujillo, La Guairá, Puerto Cabello, Cumana), and Mexico (Veracruz).

Michel's first success was in capturing a convoy of Dutch ships with a total cargo valued in the French currency of the time of about 400,000 livres.

He was last seen in April 1686 heading northeast towards Matanzas Inlet in Florida to rescue fellow French buccaneer Nicolas Brigaut, who had been grounded in a storm. The rescue never came, and Spanish soldiers captured and executed Brigaut. Grammont's ship was caught in the same storm and was never seen again.

Michel 'Le Basque' Etchegorria

Michel was one of the early buccaneers who hunted oxen and wild pigs on Hispaniola and nearby islands from around 1657. He teamed up with François l'Olonnais to ferry ground troops and to sack the cities of Maracaibo and Gibraltar in Venezuela, and while on their way to sack Maracaibo in Venezuela, they came across a Spanish treasure ship, which they captured and found a cargo of cocoa beans, gemstones, and more than 260,000 Spanish dollars (silver coins worth eight Spanish reales, hence the name 'pieces of eight').

The Spanish sent two ships to capture him, but with two small boats he boarded the much larger Spanish ships and seized them. Apparently he sent a letter to the Governor of Cartagena thanking him for providing him with such good ships.

Some say that he returned to his native homeland in the Basque Country where he was greeted and congratulated for his exploits. Some say that he returned to the Caribbean and captured a Spanish ship in Portobello, Panama in 1668, but was later killed that year leading a raiding party upriver.

Pierre 'Le Grand'

Pierre is best known for an attack on a Spanish galleon. The place and date are uncertain but it is estimated to have been around 1650 around the Caicos Islands or Cape Tiburón, western Hispaniola.

The galleon was sighted straggling from a Spanish treasure fleet, which they had spotted after a long voyage without event. They took a vote and decided to pursue it, and managed to draw alongside in the fading light of the sunset without being seen.

According to legend, Pierre ordered a hole to be cut in their own boat so that the men would fight harder with no means of retreat. They climbed the sides of the ship armed with pistols and swords. They completely overwhelmed the ship, taking the captain captive while he played cards in his cabin, seizing the gun room and killing the guards, preventing any of the crew from obtaining weapons with which to put up resistance. They had no choice but to surrender.

Some of the crew were forced into service on his ship, the rest were put ashore presumably in Hispaniola. They then took the ship and the captured men along with his crew back to France. After that he disappears from history.

Pierre le Picard

Born in 1624 in France, Pierre le Picard is first mentioned as travelling with François l'Olonnais and raiding in Maracaibo and Gibraltar in Venezuela in 1666, and Puerto Cabello in 1667 followed by San Pedro Sula in Honduras.

Along with fellow buccaneer Moïse Vauquelin he rejected l'Olonnais's plan to sail to Guatemala, they raided the coast of Costa Rica, and then Veraguas in Panama the same year. They attempted to capture the town of Nata nearby, but this was unsuccessful and after this they parted company.

He also joined Henry Morgan at Panama, and less is known of his activities after that. Some sources say he died in 1679, but Henry Morgan who by this time was acting Governor of Jamaica mentioned him as being active against English and Spanish shipping near Port Royal in 1682.

There is also mention of a 'Captain Picard' who may have been the same person sailing with Francois Grogniet, Mathurin Desmaretsz, George Dew, and Captain Townley to raid undefended Spanish settlements on the Pacific coast from which he returned to the Caribbean in 1687, eventually retiring to Canada, possibly dying around 1679.

Claes Gerritszoon Compaen

The flag of Claes Gerritszoon Compaen

The plain blue flag is Claes's alternative to the traditional Red Flag, perhaps because the royal blue symbolises the Protestant cause of fighting Catholic Spain.

His father was an alleged member of the Geuzen, who were a group of Calvinist (Protestant) nobles who opposed Spanish rule in the Netherlands. The majority of them operated successfully at sea and were called Watergeuzen. In 1572 they captured Brielle which gave them a foothold to gain territory to form the Dutch Republic in 1581.

(Note: In maps showing the political and religious divide in the region, the Spanish Netherlands (Catholic, South) are commonly shown in red, and the Dutch Republic (Protestant, North) is commonly shown in blue).

Claes was born in 1587 and went to sea at an early age giving him plenty of experience before he became a successful merchant trading along the coast of Guinea. He used his profits as a merchant to invest in ships for privateering against the Spanish, receiving a letter of marque from the Dutch Admiralty in 1621.

He later became dissatisfied with privateering for the Dutch Republic, owing to some misunderstandings about purchase of his ship, and compensation for fishing vessels that he had seized. The authorities released several of the ships he had captured.

He turned to piracy operating in the Irish Sea and the English Channel under the protection of the Governor of the Duchy of Clare with whom he was a close friend. Later on he operated in the Mediterranean along the coastal regions of North Africa also known as the Barbary Coast selling captured ships and their cargo at ports in Morocco.

He successfully captured and sold hundreds of ships, but as the size of his crew increased, he found it harder and harder to control their drunkenness and unruly behaviour.

He was able to seek a pardon, which he received in 1627 from Prince Frederik Hendrik. However, without the proceeds of piracy as an income and with less success in later years, he died in poverty in 1660 aged 73.

Edmund Cooke

The flag of Edmund Cooke

Cooke's flag is described as being red with yellow stripes and featuring a hand holding a sword. The yellow stripes are a unique addition, but the arm holding a sword was also used by the pirate Thomas Tew on a black flag.

Edmund or Edward Cooke was known to have traded in logwood (*Haematoxylum Campechianum*, literally 'bloodwood' from Campeche in southern Mexico). This was a valuable crop which was used as a natural source of dye for fabrics.

The Spanish Empire had claimed Campeche as part of the Spanish Main, and therefore any removal of logwood or any other commodity (*Frutas de las Indias*) from territory they controlled without permission was considered illegal contraband.

The Spanish did not have a strong enough naval fleet to patrol and police the entire Spanish Main, so they resorted to issuing letters of patent to their own privateers who they referred to as *guarda costa* (guards of the coast) to capture ships transporting contraband goods.

Their methods were harsh to say the least, and they soon earned a reputation for torture, forced confessions, and murder.

Cooke was captured in 1673 by Philip Fitzgerald, an Irish privateer for the Spanish with a hatred of the English. Cooke and his crew were put in a small boat with few provisions and after two months finally arrived in Jamaica.

He protested to the Spanish officials but to no avail. He then petitioned King Charles II of England for a privateering commission, which was delayed and then ultimately ignored.

By 1679 Cooke had returned to the Caribbean to collect logwood when he and his crew narrowly avoided capture and harsh treatment by Spanish warships in Aruba.

They abandoned their cargo and hid on the shore until another Spanish ship became available, which they boarded, captured, and sailed to Jamaica where they sold off the cargo.

Cooke then joined an expedition to capture ships travelling from Lima in Peru to Puerto Bello in Panama which was unsuccessful. After a series of disagreements, accusations, mutinies, and a failed raid on Arica in northern Chile, the buccaneers returned to the Caribbean in 1682 and petitioned the governor of Antigua for permission to come ashore.

This is where Edmund Cooke disappears from recorded history, except for one last mention by William Stapleton, governor of the Leeward Islands, who reports to London that he has sent a Captain by the name of Carlile out to look for him and another pirate George Bond.

3. The Black Flag and the Pirate Round

The Black Flag

The Black Flag

The traditional Red Flag of the Buccaneers was gradually replaced by the Black Flag as privateering gave way to outright piracy.

The two flags were both used in sequence, the Black Flag as a warning to surrender immediately, and if resistance was met then the Red Flag was flown as sign that they would take the ship by force with no quarter, no mercy, and no prisoners.

The Skull & Crossbones

The Skull & Crossbones

The Skull & Crossbones is the most commonly known and widely recognised symbol ever to be added to the Black Flag in association with piracy. Also referred to as a 'death's head' or '*totenkopf*' in German, the Skull and Crossbones has its origin in the Late Middle Ages as a symbol of mortality.

A genre of art referred to as '*Danse Macabre*' became popular in religious allegory. It was designed as a '*memento mori*' to remind the viewer of the fragility of earthly existence, the end of all earthly things, and the vanity of the search for glory in this earthly life, as the personification of death summons people from all walks of life, pope, emperor, king, child, and labourer alike.

The use of this symbol in the context of piracy is designed to build on this symbolism adding warning of the ferocity of the attackers, their reputation preceding them, the vanity of resistance, and the consequence of any attempt to do so.

The Jolly Roger or Old Roger

The Jolly Roger

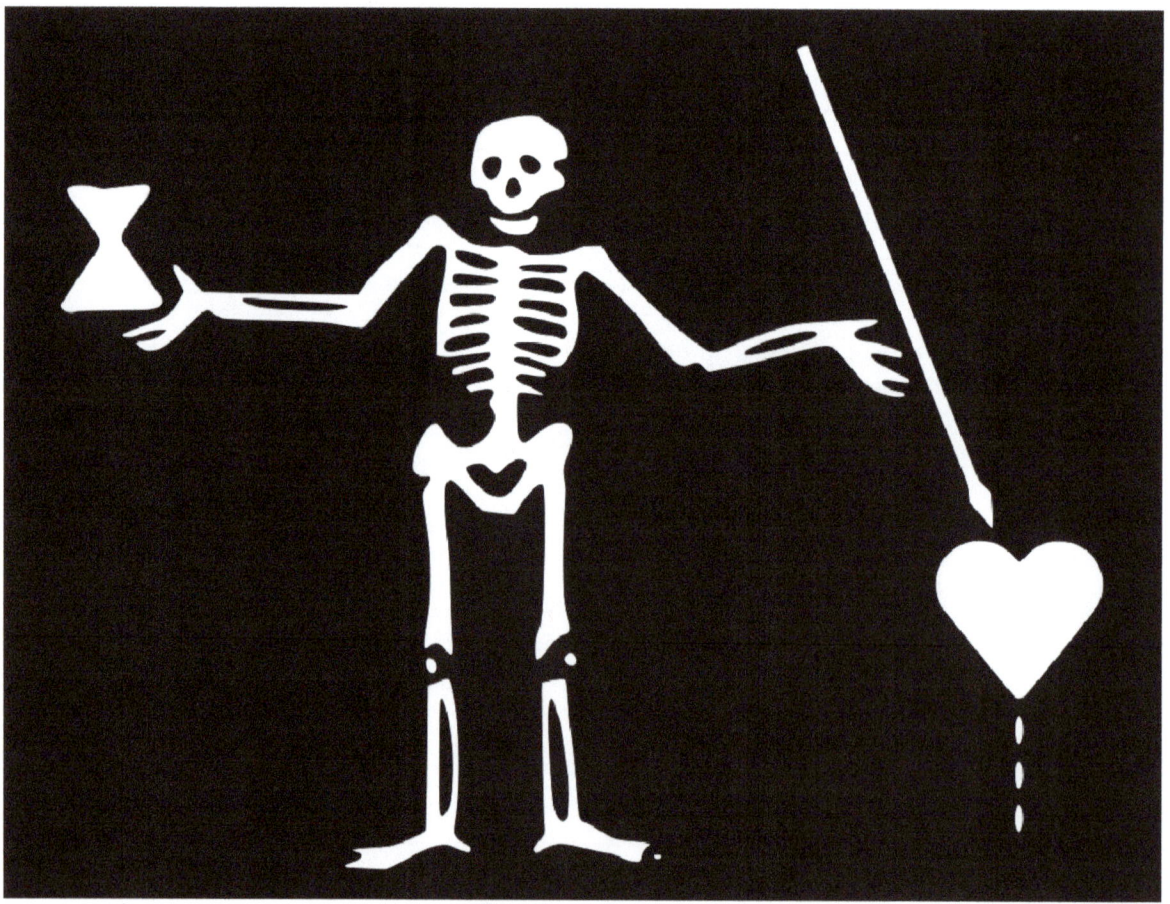

The Jolly Roger

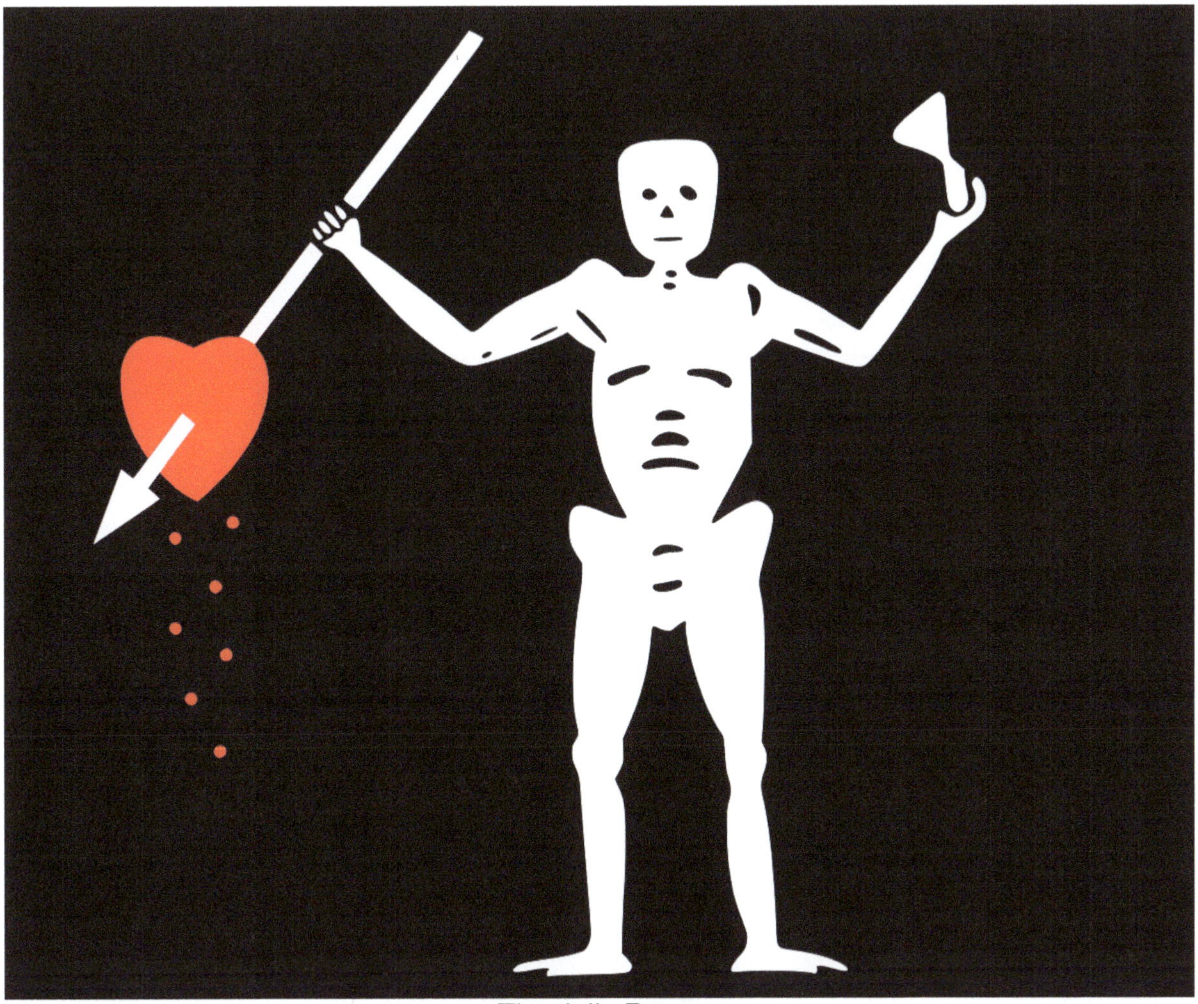

The Jolly Roger

The Jolly Roger

Several pirates of the Golden Age of Piracy are reported to have named their flag 'Jolly Roger', even though their flags were very different, which suggests that the term became a generic one used for pirate flags in general.

As well as the anglicised version of the French 'Joli Rouge' as 'Jolly Roger' it is also recorded that some pirates referred to their flag as 'Old Roger', a nickname for the devil, who was depicted in several flags with an hourglass in one hand (time is running out), and a dart or spear in the other hand striking into a heart, with three droplets of blood.

Sometimes the Old Roger is depicted in devil-like or demon-like form, sometimes as a skeleton. The hourglass, dart or spear, and bleeding heart is a common indicator that it is Old Roger, but whether a skeleton on its own can be said to be either Old Roger as the devil or a personification of death in the Danse Macabre tradition is uncertain.

The Pirate Round

Several events occurred in the late 17th century that caused many pirates to begin to look beyond the Caribbean Sea for their treasure. The English and French had become enemies again. Louis XIV of France had become the most powerful monarch of the time, and his policy of stabilising and strengthening France's frontiers was seen as a threat to the balance of power by the rest of Europe. Spain and England then effectively became allies against France who sent their navy and privateers to the Caribbean.

The Pirate Round was a sailing route pioneered by Thomas Tew in 1693 which included setting off from New York with goods to sell to the pirate settlements around Madagascar which also served as a stopping off point to repair and provision ships, then launch attacks on ships in the Indian Ocean and then distributing the goods and dividing the spoils on the return journey.

Targets included the East India Companies of Britain, France, Portugal, etc. who on their outward journey would have been laden with gold and silver, and on their return journey with fine china silks, spices, ivory, and tea.

Another option favoured by the 'Roundsmen' was to intercept Mughal merchant shipping carrying valuable goods and exotic products travelling between Surat in Gujarat, and Mecca in Saudi Arabia. Two important locations used to wait to intercept these ships were either Mocha on the Southwest coast of Yemen, or Perim Island in the Strait of Mandeb, the point at which the Gulf of Aden joins with the Red Sea, a geographical bottleneck and a strategically ideal place to launch an ambush.

The trading network that had been propped up by Frederick Philipse in New York and Adam Baldridge in Madagascar collapsed when Baldridge was forced to flee Madagascar when local tribes had learned that he had sold a group of natives as slaves, and Frederick Philipse was banned from government office for conducting a slave trade in New York. He died 4 years later.

Once news of the pirate attacks had spread Indian and Arab shipping had increased protection and convoy in co-operation with heavily armed British East India Company ships.

The War of Spanish Succession meant that there was suddenly a massive increase in demand for legally sanctioned privateers in waters closer to home.

Emanuel Wynn

The flag of Emanuel Wynn

Wynn's flag is credited with being the first known pirate flag to feature the Skull & Crossbones or 'death's head'. It also features an hourglass, a sign that for the victim time is running out and only a timely surrender will save them from death.

Some artistic interpretations of this flag feature the hourglass to the right of the Skull & Crossbones, but the commonly accepted version shows the hourglass beneath, symbolising death resting on time itself.

At the beginning of Wynn's piratical career, the English and the French had become enemies again. The French and Roman Catholic connections in the ruling House of Stuart proved unpopular with the Protestant majority in England, which ultimately brought about the downfall of the House of Stuart, which restored the traditional enmity between England and France.

As a result, in the Caribbean the cooperation that had existed between French Tortuga (Hispaniola) and English Port Royal (Jamaica) which had proved very profitable, now no longer existed.

Emanuel Wynn began raiding English merchants off the East coast of the English colony of North Carolina in the 1690s, but later moved his operations to the Caribbean Sea attacking English and Spanish ships.

On July 18th 1700 in the Cape Verde Islands off the west coast of Africa, Emanuel Wynn's pirate ship was engaged by Captain John Cranby on HMS *Poole*.

In his account in British Admiralty Records, Cranby chased Wynn into a cove at Brava Island where Wynn was able to hold out. Cranby enlisted the assistance of Portuguese soldiers, but because of their delay in attacking, Wynn sailed out of the harbour and escaped. Some say that the Portuguese soldiers' delay in attacking was deliberately designed to assist Wynn in being able to escape.

His flag was described as

> *"a sable ensign with cross bones, a death's head, and an hour glass".*

There are no reports describing any similar flag designs before this point, but 15 years later the Skull & Crossbones had become a regular feature of pirate flags, so much so that in public consciousness today, the mention of a 'Jolly Roger' conjures up the Skull & Crossbones in the imagination.

Henry Every

The main flag associated with Henry Every (also known as Henry Avery, Benjamin Bridgeman, and Long Ben) is a Skull & Crossbones with the skull in sideways profile looking to the right, wearing a kerchief and an earring. It is debated whether or not the design was on a black or red flag. Both may have been used at different times or both at once.

In the book 'A General History of the Pyrates' by Captain Charles Johnson, there is an illustration of Henry Every being escorted by a moor who is holding a parasol over his head. In the background there can be seen a flag flying with crossbones on it.

The flag of Henry Every

The flag of Henry Every

The flag of Henry Every

The flag of Henry Every

The flag of Henry Every

In the ballad 'A Copy of Verses' which was purported to the work of Henry Every, the author describes:

> *"Four Chiviligies of Gold in a bloody Field*
> *Environ'd with green, now this is my Shield*
> *Yet call out for Quarter, before you do see*
> *A bloody Flag out, which our Decree,"*

The word Chiviligies is taken to mean chevrons. This may be an attempt to link Every with the noble Every baronets, a title created in 1641 for Simon Every who was a Member of Parliament for Leicester in 1640 and a supporter of the Royalist cause in the English Civil War.

Henry Every was also given the nickname 'The Arch Pirate' or 'The King of Pirates' having been famed for pulling off one of the most significant and profitable acts of piracy ever known. He was one of the few pirates able to escape with his loot without being killed in battle or captured.

In 1695, Henry Every along with Thomas Tew, Joseph Faro, Richard Want, William Mayes, and Thomas Wake sailed to the island of Perim in the Strait of Mandeb to wait for a 25-ship convoy of Grand Mughal vessels making an annual trip to Mecca with the heavily armed treasure ship Ganj-i-Sawai. The convoy had somehow eluded them in the night, but they gave chase. Four of five days later they caught up with and captured the Ganj-i-Sawai's companion ship the Fateh Mohammed, and then a few days later the Ganj-i-Sawai itself. The opening volley took out the mainmast leaving them unable to escape, and a vicious hand to hand battle followed lasting up to three hours.

There emerged accounts of the pirates and their horrific brutality and cruelty towards the terrified survivors, resulting in the suicide of some of the women aboard to escape the prospect of barbarities that they surely would have suffered. This was corroborated by those of Every's crew who were later captured. This was not only a disaster for the convoy and the suffering of the victims onboard, but also a disaster for the relations between England and India which threatened the very existence of trade between the two countries. The Mughal Emperor was reportedly close to attacking all English persons and interests in India and driving them out altogether.

The East India company promised to pay compensation, and the Parliament declared the pirates 'hostis humani generis' (enemies of mankind) issuing a £500 bounty on Every's head, a reward which was later doubled. The first ever worldwide manhunt had begun. Every and his associates were marked men with prices on their heads.

After a deceptive bribing of the Governor of New Providence Sir Nicholas Trott, and a tip off about the coming authorities, Every's 113-person crew made their escape, with only 24 men captured, five of them were executed. Some stayed in the West Indies, some headed for North America, some to England, stopping at Ireland on the way, where suspicions were aroused while unloading their treasure, two further men were caught. Henry Every escaped and was never seen again, and no reliable account is known after June 1696. However there were stories and rumours of his being cheated out of his diamonds by merchants and dying in poverty in Devon around 1714.

Thomas Tew

The flag of Thomas Tew

The flag associated with Thomas Tew shows a white arm holding a sword, representing might and death by the sword, similar to that of Edmund Cooke's flag, but on a black background.

Thomas Tew was born around 1649, but it is not known for certain where. Some accounts suggest he was born in New England, some accounts say he was born in Maidford in Northamptonshire and emigrated to the American colonies as a child with his family. He is sometimes referred to as the Rhode Island Pirate.

He moved to Bermuda in 1691 and obtained a letter of marque from the Governor of Bermuda in 1692.

In 1693 he originally set off to attack French holdings in Gambia, but part way through the expedition he urged his crew to turn to piracy and they instead sailed to the Red Sea and seized a large dhow (trading ship) on route from India to the Ottoman Empire.

The dhow surrendered without serious resistance, and there were no casualties. Tew and the crew helped themselves to £100,000 in gold and silver as well as a large cargo ivory, spices, gemstones, and silk.

They then set a course for the Cape of Good Hope on the southwest tip of Africa, stopping off at Adam Baldridge's pirate settlement at Madagascar along the way to careen and repair.

They reached Newport in Rhode Island in 1694 and news of their successful expedition spread far and wide, and soon other pirates would try their hand at the Pirate Round.

In November 1694, Tew purchased a letter of marque from Benjamin Fletcher, royal governor of New York to prepare for privateering against the French.

In August 1695 Tew arrived at the Strait of Mandab at the mouth of the Red Sea and met with several other pirates who hoped to duplicate his success, including Henry Every, Joseph Faro, Thomas Wake, William May and Richard Want. They decided to team up and sail together to capture the Mughal treasure fleet.

Tew's ship attacked the *Fateh Muhammed*, but in the battle Tew was killed by cannon shot. The crew were demoralised and surrendered, but were later rescued by Henry Avery.

4. The High Tide

Once the War of Spanish Succession was over in 1714, thousands of sailors and privateers were relieved of their duty and were forced to look for employment elsewhere.

Some found employment on merchant ships sailing back and forth across the Atlantic Ocean with an ever increasing amount of goods. Some turned to piracy in order to attack and seize those same ships, and also to escape the harsh conditions and low wages of the navy and the merchant navy.

After a raid on Spanish divers trying to recover gold from a sunken treasure galleon near Florida in 1715, the Governor of Jamaica refused to allow the pirates to spend their loot on his island.

The Bahamas had been abandoned during the war, so a new base was set up at Nassau on the island of New Providence. This became the new port for trading stolen goods, and many taverns and brothels soon sprang up to entertain the pirates who flocked there.

For the next three years, countless goods changed hands, spoils were shared, ships were repaired, bought and sold, plans of attack were discussed and formed, news of other pirates' exploits was shared, and it became a haven for all those who sailed against the rest of the world.

In July 1718 the new Governor Woodes Rogers arrived hoping to end piracy by persuading as many pirates as he could to accept the pardon of the new King George I and end their evil ways. In doing so, Rogers hoped to be able to secure trade in the region in return for a share in the colony's profits.

Rogers had suffered great financial losses as a result of his previous privateering activities, which he had written about in his book '*A Cruising Voyage Round the World*'. The book had achieved financial success, but was not enough to pay off all of his debts.

Part of the reason for this success was his detailed account of rescuing the Scottish sailor Alexander Selkirk who had been stranded on Juan Fernández Island for four years. His story of survival caught the public interest, and was the inspiration for 'Robinson Crusoe' by Daniel Defoe.

Woodes Rogers' Governorship was under threat from the Spanish who were planning to retake the Bahamas and drive out the English, and pirate Charles Vane had threatened to team up with fellow pirate Edward 'Blackbeard' Teach to do the same, with great motivation, since the loss of Nassau as a base of operations would threaten their livelihood and existence. The stakes were high, and the fight was on.

European trade was under significant strain due to piracy, and the European nations increased their navies to give greater protection to merchants, and also to hunt down pirates. The sailors who were still without employment were recruited. This was the turning point.

Bartholomew 'Black Bart' Roberts

The flag of Bartholomew Roberts

The flag of Bartholomew Roberts

The flag of Bartholomew Roberts

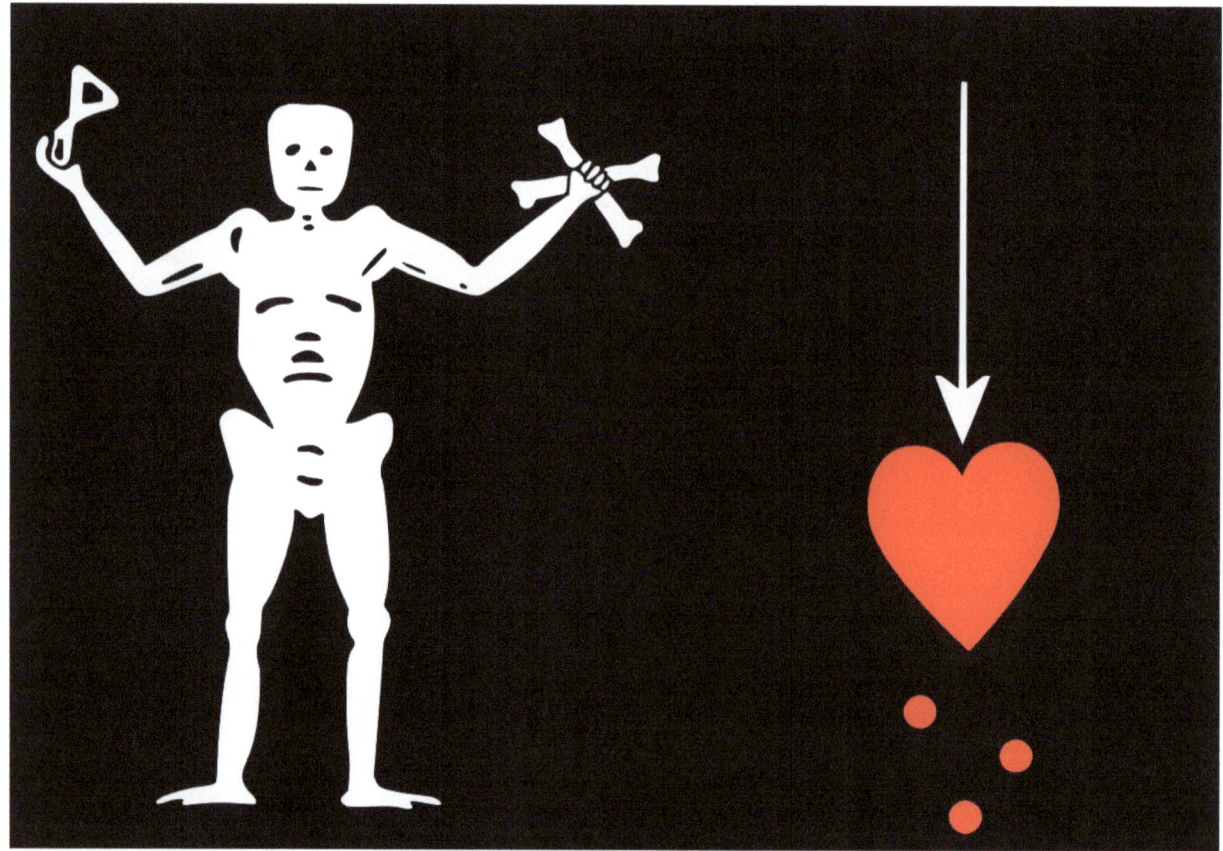
The flag of Bartholomew Roberts

The flag of Bartholomew Roberts

The flag of Bartholomew Roberts

The first flag associated with Roberts shows a depiction of Roberts himself on the left and Old Roger on the right holding a spear, and they are holding an hourglass between them.

The second flag associated with Roberts depicts him standing on two skulls with 'ABH' (A Barbadian's Head) and 'AMH' (A Martiniquian's Head) as he had sworn vengeance on these two islands. The other flags attributed to Roberts include versions of Old Roger, and also a 'death's head' and a sword.

Born John Roberts in 1682, he changed his name to Bartholomew perhaps after the well known buccaneer Bartholomew Sharp. He went to sea aged 13 and by 1718 he was mate of a ship in Barbados.

Roberts was taken under the wing of fellow Welsh pirate Howell Davies, who noticed Roberts' skills in navigating, and with whom he confided in speaking Welsh which no one else in the crew was able to understand.

When Davies was killed by a Portuguese ambush on the island of Príncipe, Roberts was elected as captain on account of his navigation skills and outspoken personality.

His next act was to command the revenge of Davis's death, which they did in the darkness of night, killing a large number of the male population, stealing anything they could carry, and capturing a Dutch slave ship in the process. The success of this raid strengthened the crew's loyalty to Roberts.

In 1720 the inhabitants of Barbados sent two ships to hunt pirates. They encountered Roberts and his crew in the ship *Fortune* and French pirate Montigny la Palisse and his crew in the ship *Sea King*.

Sea King quickly turned and sailed away and *Fortune* sustained considerable damage in the engagement and had to break off, heading for Hispaniola to repair, losing twenty of the crew to their wounds on the way. Later Roberts also learned that there were two ships from Martinique on the lookout for pirates as well, and it is at this point he designed his second flag (see above).

After raids in Newfoundland, the Caribbean, and West Africa, Roberts' was warned by retired pirate John 'Old Crackers' Leadstone that two Royal Navy ships HMS *Swallow* and HMS *Weymouth* had out looking for him and would return before Christmas.

In January 1722 Roberts and his fleet sailed into Ouidah (Whydah) harbour and took 10 of the 11 ships anchored in the harbour by ransom. The master of the 11th ship refused the terms, and their ship was set on fire. The ships were slave ships, and the ship that had been set on fire had approximately eighty slaves on board, who all died by fire, drowning, or shark attack after jumping overboard.

Finally when HMS *Swallow* returned, Roberts' crew were drunk and unfit for battle. Roberts dressed in his finest clothes as he was known to do before battle.

After two broadsides from HMS *Swallow* Roberts was killed by a blast of grapeshot which hit him in the throat as he stood on deck. His wish was to be buried at sea, and this was quickly carried out before his body could be captured by HMS *Swallow*. His body was never found.

Captain Napin

The flag of Captain Napin

The flag of Captain Napin

Captain Napin's flag is described by a sailor called Nathaniel Brooker who was aboard a ship called *Restoration* in 1717. The ship was seized by Napin and Thomas Nichols, and was stripped of everything of any use, even down to kettles and frying pans. In Brooker's account he described Napin's flag as follows:

> *"He had in his flag a death's head and an hourglass".*

While his first name is not known, Captain Napin or Napping is best known for sailing alongside Benjamin Hornigold in the Caribbean and the American east coast.

They captured several vessels near Jamaica and Puerto Bello in Panama, but they were chased away by HMS *Winchelsea* near Cuba. Napin and Hornigold parted company afterwards, sometimes sailing together until October of that year. Napin also attacked another ship named *Adventure* in September of 1717 and a ship's tender (a vessel used to transport people or supplies to larger ships) near Trinidad in October 1717.

In early 1718, Captain Vincent Pearse of HMS *Phoenix* arrived in Nassau to bring the news that King George I of England had offered a pardon for pirates who would give up piracy and surrender by September. The pardon would later be delivered and enforced by Governor of the Bahamas, Captain Woodes Rogers.

Thomas Nichols and Benjamin Hornigold had accepted the pardon, but Napin never arrived at Nassau to be pardoned. It is not known whether or not he failed to attend because he decided against surrender, or because he had not heard the news. He was last seen and reported as sailing between Brazil and the African coast in March 1718, but after that, no record of his activities exists.

Perhaps he settled somewhere on the African west coast, or perhaps Île Sainte-Marie off Madagascar, perhaps he decided to disappear and escape the profession of piracy for good, we may never know.

Charles Harris

Charles Harris's flag is described in several sources matching the depiction of Old Roger.

From Captain Charles Johnson's 'A General History of the Pyrates':

> *"A Day or two after they parted, Spriggs was chosen Captain by the rest, and a black Ensign was made, which they called Jolly Roger, with the same Device that Captain Low carried, viz. a white Skeliton in the Middle of it, with a Dart in one Hand striking a bleeding Heart, and in the other, an Hour-Glass; when this was finished and hoisted, they fired all their Guns to salute their Captain and themselves, and then looked out for Prey".*

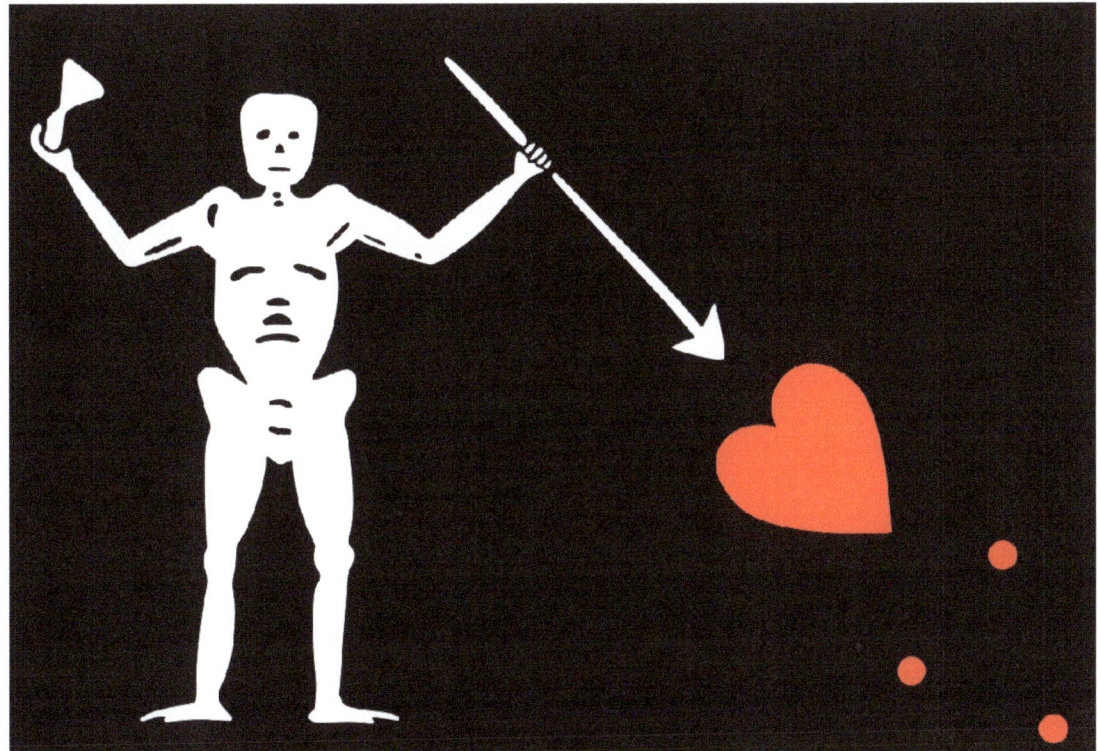

The flag of Charles Harris

From another source claiming a blue field instead of black:

> *"...under their own deep Blew Flagg which was hoisted up on their Gallows, and had pourtraied on the middle of it, an Anatomy with an Hour-Glass in one hand, and a dart in the Heart with 3 drops of blood proceeding from it, in the other".*

Charles Harris became a pirate in 1722 when his logwood hauling ship *Greyhound* was captured by George Lowther aboard the *Happy Delivery* between Honduras and Boston. Because of their initial resistance, many of the crew of the *Greyhound* were killed.

Harris was among those who survived and was forced aboard the *Happy Delivery* to join the crew where he willingly signed Lowther's pirate code to join.

Harris sailed with Lowther, Edward Low, and Francis Spriggs, which explains why their flags are of a similar common design by accounts.

On the 10th June 1723 Edward Low attacked what he thought was a whaling ship off Delaware Bay. It was actually the Royal Navy man-of-war HMS *Greyhound* under Captain Peter Slogard. The resulting combat lasted several hours.

Low's ship *Fancy* was damaged but escaped carrying £150,000 in gold, while Harris's ship was defeated and surrendered. They were taken to stand trial and Harris and over 25 others were hanged on 19th July 1723.

A local newspaper of the day, The New England Courant, reported:

> *"Their Black Flag, with the Pourtrature of Death having an Hour-Glass in one Hand, and a Dart in the other, at the end of which was the Form of a Heart with three Drops of Blood, falling from it, was affix'd at one Corner of the Gallows. This Flag they call'd Old Roger, and often used to say they would live and die under it".*

Christopher Condent

The flag of Christopher Condent

The flag associated with Christopher Condent has three Skull & Crossbones, sometimes on a rectangular flag, sometimes on a fanion or pennant (triangular flag).

Pirates often used an alias, and Christopher Condent's real name is uncertain. Alternative first names include William, Edmond, Edward, or John. Alternative surnames include Congdon, Coudon, Connor or Condell, and also the nickname 'Billy One-Hand'.

Upon the arrival of Woodes Rogers as Governor of the Bahamas and his efforts to suppress piracy, Condent and his crew left New Providence and sailed to the Cape Verde Islands off the coast of West Africa where they captured a ship carrying a cargo of Portuguese wine.

They then sailed to Brazil and took more ships as prizes. Either Condent or members of his crew are reported to have cut off the ears and noses of some of the Portuguese prisoners. It is unclear whether this was a form of punishment to deter the prisoners who may have been ringleaders in plotting to mount a resistance and take over the ship, or outright savagery without any cause other than boredom and cruelty.

Returning to Cape Verde, Condent and his crew captured a flotilla of ships, and a Dutch warship off the Island of Santiago. The warship was renamed *The Fiery Dragon*.

In 1719, Condent reached Madagascar and established a base on the island of Île Sainte-Marie with John Halsey, Edward England, and John Taylor. Madagascar had been used as a base since the 'Pirate Round' period to attack targets in the Indian Ocean and ships of the East India Company.

The Royal Navy were around the Indian Ocean more frequently, which increased the risk of capture.

After plundering more ships and dividing the spoils, in 1721 Condent and some of his crew sailed to the island of Bourbon and negotiated a pardon from the French governor.

Half of the men settled on the island, and Condent even married the Governor's sister-in-law. In 1723 he travelled to France with his wife and settled in Brittany as a wealthy merchant.

He is one of the few pirates who have been able to retire before being killed in battle or tried and hanged.

Christopher Moody and William Moody

The flag of Christopher Moody

The flag of Christopher Moody

The flag of William Moody

The flag of William Moody

The flag associated with Christopher Moody has a winged hourglass, an arm holding a sword, and a Skull & Crossbones with the bones crossed behind the skull. Sometimes this is shown on a red flag, sometimes a black flag.

The flags associated with William Moody are a pierced heart and an Old Roger.

Christopher and William Moody have been confused with each other in various accounts mentioning only a 'Captain Moody'.

The two Moodys could have crossed paths at one time when Christopher Moody was a member of Howell Davis's crew, and Davis teamed up with fellow pirates Thomas (Jeremiah) Cocklyn and Olivier Levasseur. Cocklyn had been a member of William Moody's crew but was later marooned following an unsuccessful mutiny.

William Moody commanded one or two ships and plundered vessels off the coast of the Carolinas, and these actions are often attributed to Christopher Moody

In December of 1718 they seized ships near St Thomas and held their captains hostage and threatened to burn their ships unless they pirates were given supplies. As a result, the Governor of St Thomas asked for an additional warship to protect against the pirates.

William Moody was one of the many pirates to have accepted the King's pardon before September 1718, but likely returned to piracy shortly afterwards and is believed to have died in 1719.

Christopher Moody is known to have operated at least until 1722 until he was captured alongside Bartholomew Roberts by the Royal Navy HMS *Swallow* captained by Chaloner Ogle.

While Bartholomew Roberts was killed in battle, Christopher Moody was later hanged at Cape Coast Castle along with Thomas Sutton and other members of Bartholomew Roberts' crew. The death of Bartholomew Roberts is considered as the beginning of the end of the Golden Age of Piracy.

The flag associated with Christopher Moody was first described in the mid 18th century, and artistic representations of the flag began to appear in various books around the early 20th Century.

Edward 'Blackbeard' Teach

The flag of Edward 'Blackbeard' Teach

Edward Teach (also known as Thatch) is believed to have flown at least two different flags, the Old Roger and the Skull & Crossbones, perhaps both at the same time.

Teach was born around 1680 and may have sailed on privateer ships during the war of 1702-1713 known as 'Queen Anne's War', which is sometimes regarded as the theatre of war for the War of Spanish Succession, but sometimes regarded as a standalone conflict, in which Spanish Florida and the English Province of Carolina attacked each other, while the English fought French colonists at Mobile, Alabama. Each side included Native American allies.

After the war, Teach settled in New Providence in the Bahamas and joined the crew of Benjamin Hornigold who gave him command of a sloop that he had captured. They seized a ship sailing out of Havana carrying 120 barrels of flour, and then took a ship from Bermuda with 100 barrels of wine. Near Cape Charles in Virginia they seized the ship *Betty* and took only her cargo of Madeira wine before sinking her.

Teach then captured a French slave ship known as *La Concorde* and renamed her *Queen Anne's Revenge*, and with 40 guns and a crew of over 300 men he became a well renowned pirate.

The flag of Edward 'Blackbeard' Teach

The nickname 'Blackbeard' was given to him on account of his thick black beard and intimidating presence. He reportedly lit slow matches and placed them under his hat to make himself appear even more frightening to those he robbed, relying less on violence and more on appearance.

In May 1718 Teach's flotilla blockaded the port of Charles Town in the Province of South Carolina. All vessels coming in and out were stopped. The town had no guard ship, and so for the next five or six days about nine vessels were ransacked.

The *Crowley* was heading for London when it was stopped by Teach, the passengers were held for ransom in return for medical supplied which they badly needed. Teach threatened to execute all the passengers of the *Crowley*, to send their heads to the Governor, and to burn all the captured ships. The demands were met, and the prisoners were released, after being relieved of their valuables and in some cases clothing.

He accepted a royal pardon at Bath Town in North Carolina, but soon returned to piracy again, where he attracted attention from Alexander Spotswood, the Governor of Virginia. Spotswood arranged for a party of soldiers and sailors to capture Blackbeard and his crew.

Lieutenant Robert Maynard attacked Teach at Ocracoke Inlet on 22nd November 1718 and after a fearsome battle Teach was surrounded and isolated on deck by Maynard's men, and as he lunged forward to attack Maynard he was slashed across the neck by one of Maynard's men. Badly wounded, he was then attacked and killed by several more of Maynard's crew. Later examination of Teach's body revealed that he had been shot five times and cut about twenty times.

His head was severed and hung from the bowsprit of Maynard's ship so that the reward for his head could be collected. The remaining pirates were caught, imprisoned, tried, and hanged.

Edward England

The flag of Edward England

The flag of Edward England

There are two flags associated with Edward England, the Skull & Crossbones, almost exactly the same as that flown by Samuel 'Black Sam' Bellay, and the other flag shows a skull wearing a tricorn hat in sideways profile similar to that of Henry Every's flag, but with crossed swords, similar to those on John 'Calico Jack' Rackham's flag.

Edward England was born Edward Seegar around 1685 in Ireland. He made his way to Jamaica and served as a privateer during the War of Spanish Succession. He was captured by the pirate captain Christopher Winter and forced to join his crew. Winter took England to the pirate base at Nassau in The Bahamas.

In 1715 he took part in Henry Jennings' expedition to Palma de Ayz in Florida. The Spanish had set up a salvage camp there and were attempting to recover treasure from a sunken fleet that was lost off the Florida coast in a hurricane after departing from Havana, Cuba to Spain.

In March 1718 England was reported as Charles Vane's quartermaster, when the Royal Navy captured Vane's ship *Lark*, but the crew were released to encourage them to accept the Kind's pardon, and spread the news among the rest of the pirate community to do the same.

England and Vane decided not to accept the pardon. By the time Governor Woodes Rogers arrived in Nassau, England was made captain of his own ship, and they set sail for the cost of Africa.

On the way to Africa they captured the ship *Cadogan* from Bristol. England offered the crew a choice to join his crew. One of the crew was Howell Davis, who refused to sign the pirate code and join. England refused to kill him, and instead gave him command of the captured ship, beginning the start of Davis's pirate career.

While plundering a town in Southern Africa, England saw a beautiful woman by the name of Amy Brionso. He kidnapped her and kept her in his captain's quarters. England comforted her and she gradually fell in love with him.

They married and had a son they named John Edward England. Concerned for her safety and the safety of their son, England left them on the eastern coast of South Africa. He asked Amy to instruct their son John to name his first born son Edward after him, with the hope that it would become a family tradition.

England had a good nature and a kindness towards his captors that did not always go down well with those under his command. When England attacked a ship *Cassandra* of the East India Company in the Indian Ocean under the command of James McCrae, a long bloody battle ensued until both ships ran aground.

Ninety of England's crew had died in the battle. England ordered McCrae's life spared. This angered some of the crew, particularly a John Taylor who organised a vote to remove England as captain.

England was removed as captain and marooned without sufficient provisions on Mauritius with three other loyal crew members. They scavenged to survive, and eventually they built a small boat and sailed to St Augustine's Bay in Madagascar, where England died in late 1720 or early 1721.

Edward 'Ned' Low

The flag of Edward 'Ned' Low

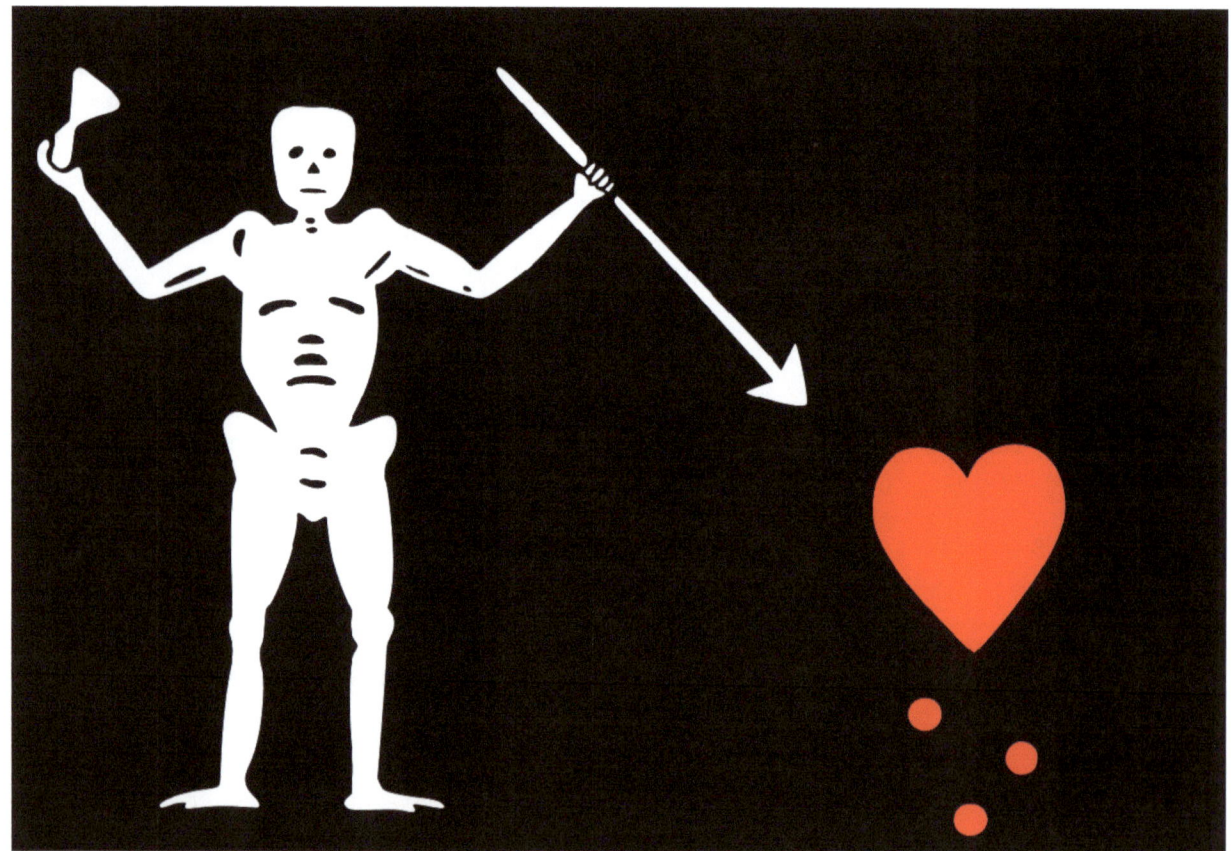
The flag of Edward 'Ned' Low

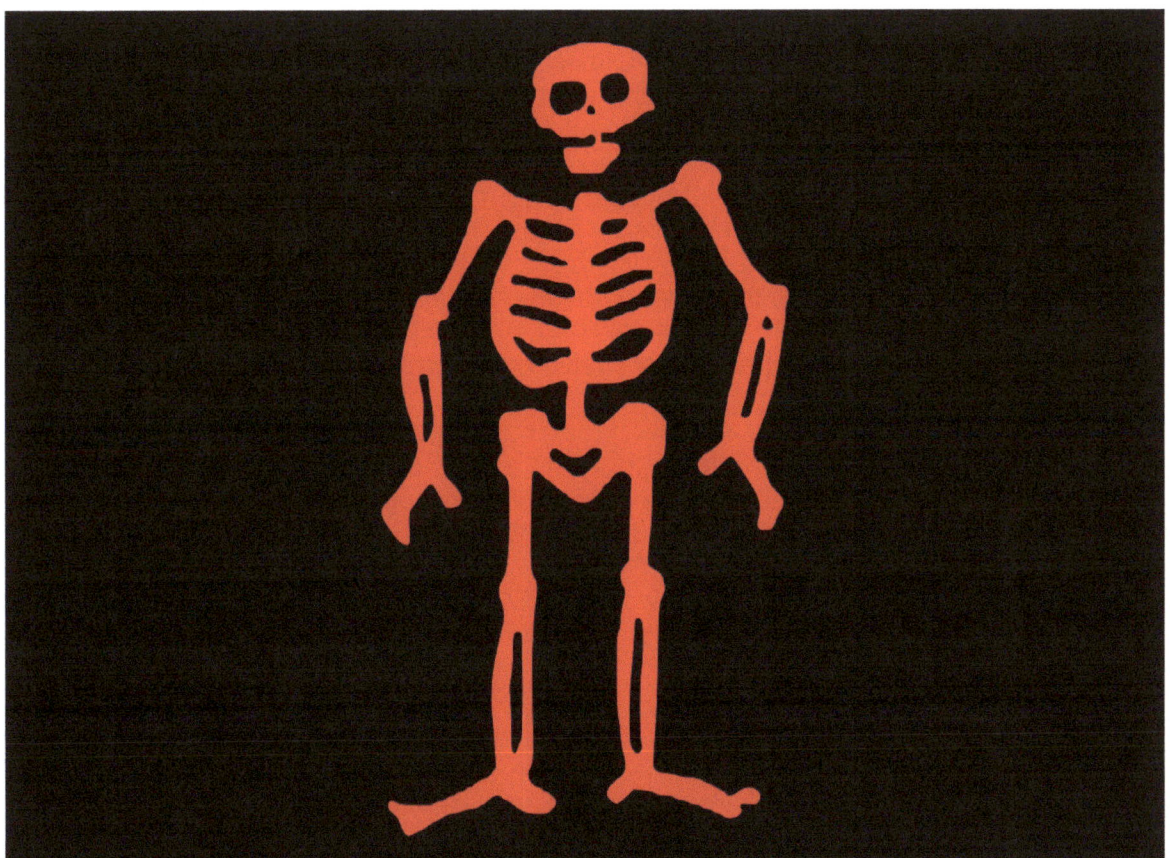
The flag of Edward 'Ned' Low

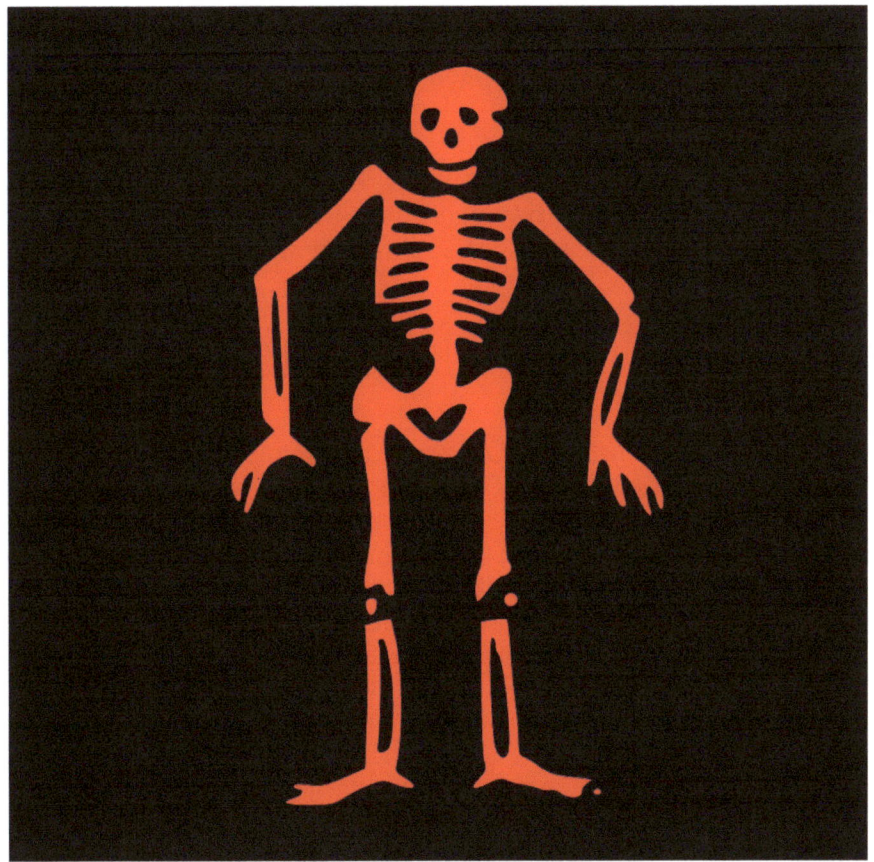
The flag of Edward 'Ned' Low

There are several different styles of flag associated with Edward Low. A trumpeter in gold on a green background which he used to call his fleet's captains to meetings aboard the flagship, an Old Roger similar to that of Edward 'Blackbeard' Teach, and a red skeleton on a black background which he first flew in late July 1723, and became notorious, with his quarrelsome nature and reputation for cruelty.

Low (sometimes Lowe or Loe) was born into poverty around 1690 in Westminster, London, where he was a thief from an early age. He moved to Boston Massachusetts as a young man, where he married Eliza Marble. They had a son who died in infancy, and then a daughter called Elizabeth born in 1719. Eliza died in childbirth, leaving Low with his daughter who he left behind.

At first Low worked as a rigger joining a gang of twelve men heading for Honduras where they planned to collect a shipment of logs for resale in Boston.

One day he returned to the ship when hungry, but was told by the captain that he would have to wait to eat and make do with a ration of rum. He reportedly took up a loaded musket and fired at the captain but missed, hitting another poor fellow through the throat.

He was forced to leave the boat with his friends, including Francis Spriggs. They took over a small ship off the coast of Rhode Island, determined to set sail under a black flag and declare war against the world.

Low and his crew seized a ship on the popular shipping route between New York and Boston. He then headed south and began operating around the Cayman Islands, sailing with pirate George Lowther. Their crew was continually expanded by desperate sailors wishing to join him.

It is around this time that Low had begun to show a taste for cruelty, teaching a technique of torture to Francis Spriggs involving tying rope between a victim's fingers and then setting it alight, burning the fingers to the bone.

Lowther captured a ship named *Rebecca* and gave it to Low to captain, and they amicably dissolved their partnership.

Low then captured thirteen fishing vessels of New England, all of whom surrendered without resistance. The ships were looted and burned except for the largest which was renamed The Fancy and became Low's flagship. He surprised his victims by flying false colours while approaching unsuspecting vessels.

As his taste for cruelty grew worse, his crew refused to follow his orders, and George Lowther and Francis Spriggs parted company with him.

Some say that Low was last sighted near the Canaries and Guinea, some say that he sailed for Brazil when his ship sank with the loss of all hands. The National Maritime Museum in London states that he was never caught, ending his days in Brazil.

Another account suggests that Low was the subject of a mutiny in which he was set adrift by his crew later being rescued by a French ship, and when the French authorities realised who he was, he was brought to trial and hanged in Martinique in 1724.

Francis Spriggs

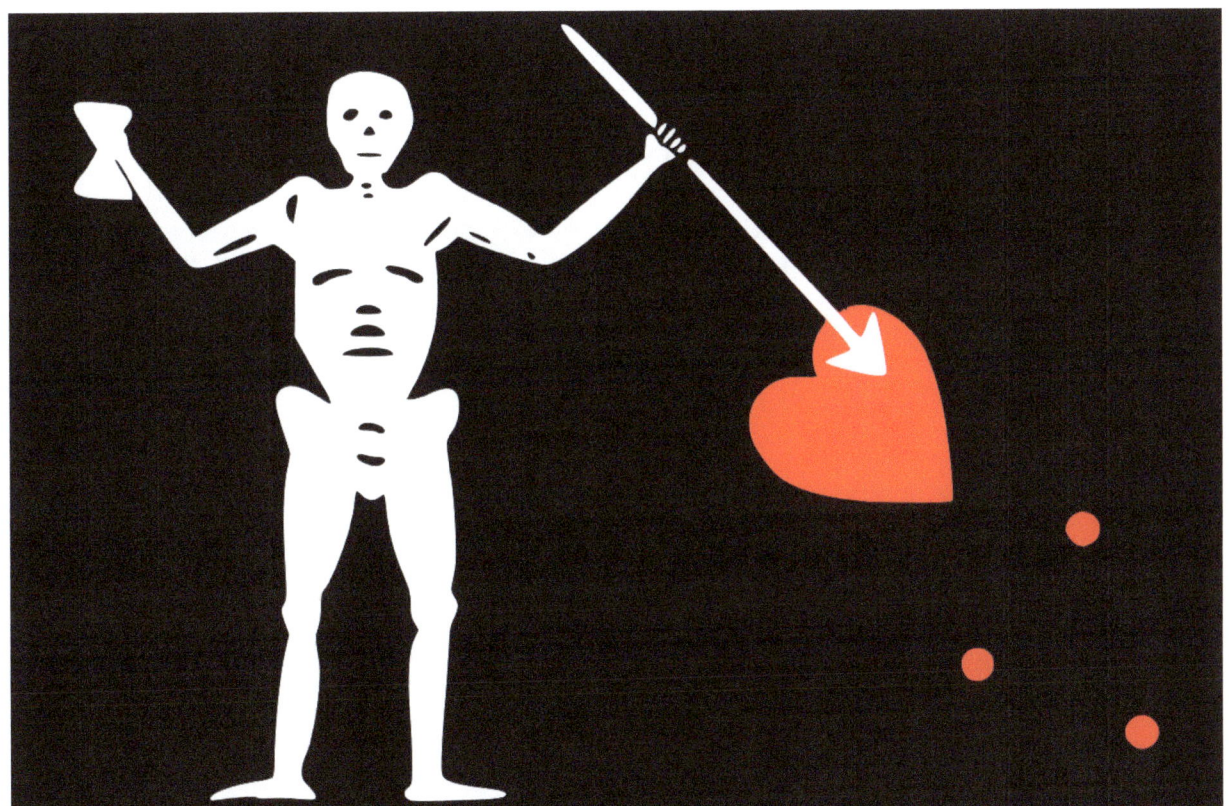

The flag of Francis Spriggs

The flag of Francis Spriggs is based on the Old Roger, similar to that flown by Edward Teach, Edward Low, and Charles Harris.

Spriggs was associated with George Lowther and Edward Low and was active in the Caribbean and the Bay of Honduras in the early 1720s.

Spriggs and Lowther appear to have had a falling out with Low over the disciplining of one of the crew around Christmas 1724, after which they sailed away and deserted Low that night.

Some of the crews that were captured by Spriggs were subjected to a form of torture known as 'the sweats', involving the crewman being placed in the middle of a circle of lit candles around the mast, and being made to run around the mast while the pirates poked and jabbed at them with knives and forks as a kind of 'running the gauntlet'.

Spriggs and his crew then captured a ship near St Lucia which was captained by a merchant from Martinique carrying logwood. After taking as much as they could carry from the ship, they threw the cargo of logwood into the sea.

Next they sailed to Roatán near the Bay of Honduras where they anchored. Spriggs ordered their prisoners from captured ships to be put ashore. Many of these prisoners are said to have displayed wounds inflicted upon them by the pirates during their captivity.

On the 4th July 1724, Spriggs and his crew captured a ship near Bermuda and tortured the captives by hoisting them as high as the tops of the sails and then dropping them against the deck.

The cruelty that Spriggs showed to his captors is very different from the mere threat of violence and cruelty that pirates such as Edward Teach were able to impose upon their captors by their intimidating presence in order to make them cooperate and surrender. Some pirates were as cruel as they needed to be, as a last resort, whereas some pirates were as cruel as they could be, as a first resort.

Spriggs the made several trips to the Bay of Honduras capturing at least another 30 more ships while managing to escape several attempts to capture him.

In one account Francis Spriggs, Edward Low, Richard Shipton, and another pirate named Cooper were captured by HMS *Diamond* and HMS *Spence*. Some say that Spriggs and Low were marooned while en route back to Jamaica, where they were killed by indigenous Miskito peoples, while Cooper blew up his own ship with gunpowder rather than be captured.

Another account suggests that Spriggs and Low escaped again, and no more is known about Spriggs' activities after that.

George Lowther

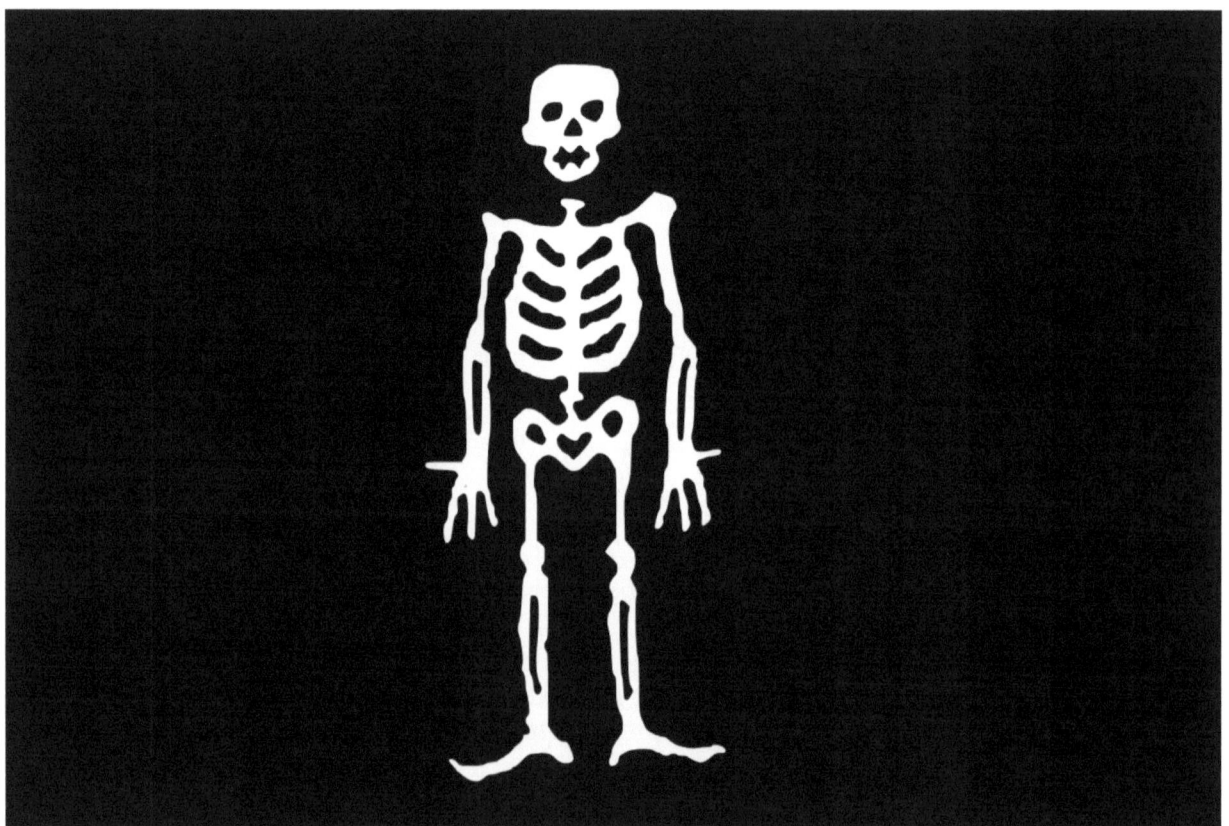

The flag of George Lowther

The flag associated with George Lowther is a skeleton or Old Roger. Sometimes in accounts of the time, the skeleton is described as an 'anatomy'.

George Lowther was second mate on a slave ship *Gambia Castle* under the command of Captain Charles Russell. Lowther was more popular with the crew, and Russell distrusted him, and attempted to have him flogged many of the crew defended Lowther which caused division among the crew.

Captain John Massey was also on board the *Gambia Caste* along with a group of soldiers under his command. Lowther and Massey set sail while Russell was offboard, leaving him behind. Massey intended to return to England, but everyone else disagreed. Lowther was made captain and renamed the ship *Delivery*.

After capturing several ships, another disagreement arose about whether or not to loot a village on shore. Lowther obtained a smaller ship which he named *Happy Delivery* and Lowther and Massey went their separate ways. He left the Carolinas and later developed a tactic of ramming his ship into another while his crew boarded and looted it.

They sailed to the Grand Caymans where they met the ship Greyhound captained by Benjamin Edwards, a sea captain and merchant from Boston. Lowther fired a cannon as a signal, to which Edwards responded with a broadside. The pirates boarded the *Greyhound*, killed all on board, and burnt the ship.

Lowther also gave his lieutenant Edward Low command of a captured ship called *Rebecca*, after which Low left to begin his own career as a pirate captain.

Lowther sailed his fleet to Guatemala, where they were attacked by indigenous peoples. He was forced to leave some ships and men behind. His crew and supplies were transferred to the ship *Revenge*.

In 1722 Lowther sailed to the island of Blanquilla, but was spotted by Walter Moore of the HMS *Eagle*. Lowther was able to escape to the island by exiting the ship via the cabin window along with 12 others. Only four made it to shore, and after a search, Lowther's body was found. He had apparently shot himself in the head rather than be taken prisoner.

Jean Thomas Dulaien

The flag of Jean Thomas Dulaien

The flag of Jean Thomas Dulaien

The flag of Jean Thomas Dulaien

The first flag associated with Jean Thomas Dulaien is a combination of the Skull & Crossbones (or a severed head with crossbones) and Old Roger, a flag which is also attributed to Walter Kennedy. The second flag features three skulls, a sword, crossbones, and two hourglasses.

Jean Thomas Dulaien (Dulaiën or du Lain) was born in 1704 and received a respectable education in France, and became a licensed ship's pilot. He began privateering in the Caribbean around 1727 searching for English ships.

His crew was a mixture of French and Spanish sailors. After a disagreement between the French and the Spanish crew, the French mutinied and either massacred the Spanish, or beat them and threw them overboard, depending in different accounts. Dulaien was elected captain and their ship was renamed '*Sans Pitie*' ('without pity' or 'merciless').

With Tortuga, Port Royal, and Nassau no longer available as a haven for privateers, corsairs, flibustiers, and pirates, Dulaien set up a base of operations on the island of West Caicos, approximately 170km north of Tortuga. From there Dulaien and his crew preyed on merchants travelling through the Caicos Passage.

The crew agreed on their own pirate code or articles of agreement, which included rules regarding the punishment of crew members who deserted, sequestered loot for themselves, or failed in their duty. Like other pirate codes they also agreed on compensation for crew who were injured. Killing prisoners was strictly prohibited, unless they were Spanish.

The pirate code of Dulaien and his crew also included rules of engagement such as when they would give quarter. For example, if a ship resisted once their black flag was flown, they would raise the red flag, effectively their last warning. If more than three cannon shots were heard after that, then they would take the ship by force and no one would be spared.

Within a few months they had acquired an impressive fleet, and a great deal of wealth. At this point Dulaien and his crew decided to quit while they were ahead, or get out while the going was good, divide their loot and head back to France in the hope of gaining a pardon from King Louis XV.

Once Dulaien's ship was seized by the authorities much of the valuable cargo was missing, resulting in the crew being arrested. The threat of excommunication to anyone who withheld information on the location of the valuables proved effective in tracing the treasure. After subsequent appeals they were released again.

Captain Dulaien himself however was left in jail for some time afterwards, and what became of him after that is not known.

Jeremiah Cocklyn

The flag of Jeremiah Cocklyn

The first flag associated with Jeremiah Cocklyn has an arm holding a dagger similar to that of Edmund Cooke, and Thomas Tew, and a Skull & Crossbones with an hourglass underneath similar to that of Emanuel Wynn.

Jeremiah Cocklyn, also known as Thomas Cocklyn, was active from 1717 to 1719. He sailed with Howell Davis, Olivier Levasseur, Richard Taylor, and William Moody. He was one of many pirates who accepted the King's pardon, but later returned to piracy. Aboard the ship *Rising Sun* he led an unsuccessful mutiny against William Moody and was marooned. Some of Moody's crew were unhappy about Moody's treatment of Cocklyn and in turn marooned Moody with 12 of his loyal crew members. Olivier Levasseur was then elected captain of *Rising Sun*.

The flag of Jeremiah Cocklyn

The second flag associated with Cocklyn shows a skeleton or Old Roger on the left, with a Skull & Crossbones and hourglass on the right as in the previous flag.

Cocklyn was known for his difficult character, and his cruelty. He was known to punish his crew by caning them, and frequently tortured his captives. He frequently argued with his fellow captains Howell Davis and Olivier Levasseur and they went their separate ways. Cocklyn carried on with his acts of piracy around the coast of Africa, and by 1720 he was reported to be at Madagascar where he is believed to have died shortly after.

John 'Calico Jack' Rackham

The flag of John 'Calico Jack' Rackham

John Rackham was known as 'Calico Jack' because of the calico clothing he used to wear (Jack is a nickname for John). His flag is a variation on the Skull & Crossbones, but with crossed swords instead of bones, similar to the design of Edward England's second flag.

Rackham was born in 1682 and little is known about his early life. He served as quartermaster to Charles Vane on the ship *Ranger* in 1718 operating out of New Providence Island in the Bahamas which had become known as The Pirate Republic.

After robbing several ships outside New York, they then were pursued by a French warship that was twice their size. Rackham was in favour of fighting the ship because it would have plenty of riches. Vane ordered a tactical withdrawal in spite of the fact that the vote was approximately 5 to 1 against him in favour of attacking. He ruled that his decision as captain was final.

Rackham called a vote in which Vane was branded as a coward and removed as captain along with his 15 supporters, and placed in another ship of the fleet with ammunition and goods.

The merchant ship *Kingston* which had a very rich cargo and promised to be an impressive haul was taken by Rackham and his crew. However, the ship was taken within sight of Port Royal, and the merchants who witnessed from shore were outraged. They sent bounty hunters to go after him, and in

February 1719 while anchored at Isla de los Pinos off Cuba, Rackham's crew were on shore. They avoided capture by hiding in the woods, but the prize ship and its rich cargo were taken away.

Rackham and his crew avoided capture by a Spanish warship on the coast of Cuba refitting their ship. The Spanish warship sailed into the harbour with a small English ship they had captured. The Spanish could see Rackham and his crew and recognised them as pirates but could not get to them as the tide was low. They anchored in the harbour entrance and waited until morning.

That night, Rackham and his crew rowed over to the captured English ship and overpowered the Spanish guards onboard. The following morning, the Spanish warship opened fire with their cannons on Rackham's old ship which was now empty, as Rackham and his crew sailed past them in their new ship and slipped away to escape.

They made their way back to Nassau in the hope of securing a royal pardon from Governor Woodes Rogers, claiming that Charles Vane had forced them into piracy. Rogers hated Vane and was inclined to believe Rackham and grant the pardon.

Anne Bonny

Anne Bonny was born around 1697 in Ireland, and moved to London, and then the Province of Carolina around 1707. She had fiery red hair and some say a fiery temper. She married a poor sailor and small-time pirate James Bonny sometime between 1714 and 1718. Anne's father disapproved of her husband and disowned her. The couple moved to Nassau where Anne would later meet Jack Rackham.

Jack Rackham and Anne Bonny began an affair. Her husband James Bonny was employed by Governor Rogers as an informant, and when he found out about the affair, he brought Anne in front of Governor Rogers who ordered her to be whipped on charges of adultery. Rackham offered to buy Anne in a 'Divorce by Purchase', but James refused.

Anne Bonny and Jack Rackham fled Nassau, and with a new crew they escaped to sea together in a ship stolen from a John Ham, which effectively made Rackham's pardon null and void. They sailed the Caribbean for several months seizing ships, often inviting the captured crews to join them.

Mary Read

Mary Read was born around 1685 and was dressed as a boy from an early age by her mother in order to secure inheritance money from her late husband's mother. Mary found work as a foot-boy (a male domestic worker) and then as a worker on a ship.

She later joined the British military which was allied with the Dutch forces fighting against the French. Read proved herself in battle, but fell in love with a Flemish soldier who she married. He died prematurely, and upon his death, Mary resumed male dress and military service in the Netherlands, but in peace time there were no prospects for advancement, and so she left and boarded a ship bound for the West Indies.

Read's ship was taken by pirates, whom she willingly joined. She accepted the King's pardon around 1718-1719 and then took a commission as a privateer. She took part in the resulting mutiny. In 1720 she joined Jack Rackham and Anne Bonny who both believed that she was a man.

Anne Bonny found herself attracted to Mary Read, and revealed to her that she was actually a woman, to which Mary responded by confiding that she too was also a woman. This was revealed to Jack Rackham and it is very likely that a three way relationship evolved.

On the 15th November 1720 Rackham and his crew were taken by surprise and captured on the west coast of Jamaica by pirate hunter Captain Jonathan Barnet. They were arrested and brought to trial for acts of piracy and sentenced to be hanged. Anne Bonny and Mary Read claimed that they were both pregnant and received a temporary stay of execution.

Mary Read died of a fever while in prison and was buried on the 28th April 1721. There is no record of the burial of her baby, which suggests that she may have died while pregnant.

There is no record of Anne Bonny's release, execution, or death, which has led to speculation about what became of her. It is now known how or when Anne Bonny died.

Jack Rackham was hanged in Port Royal on 18th November 1720, and his body was then put on public display on a gibbet as a warning to others tempted by piracy.

John Phillips

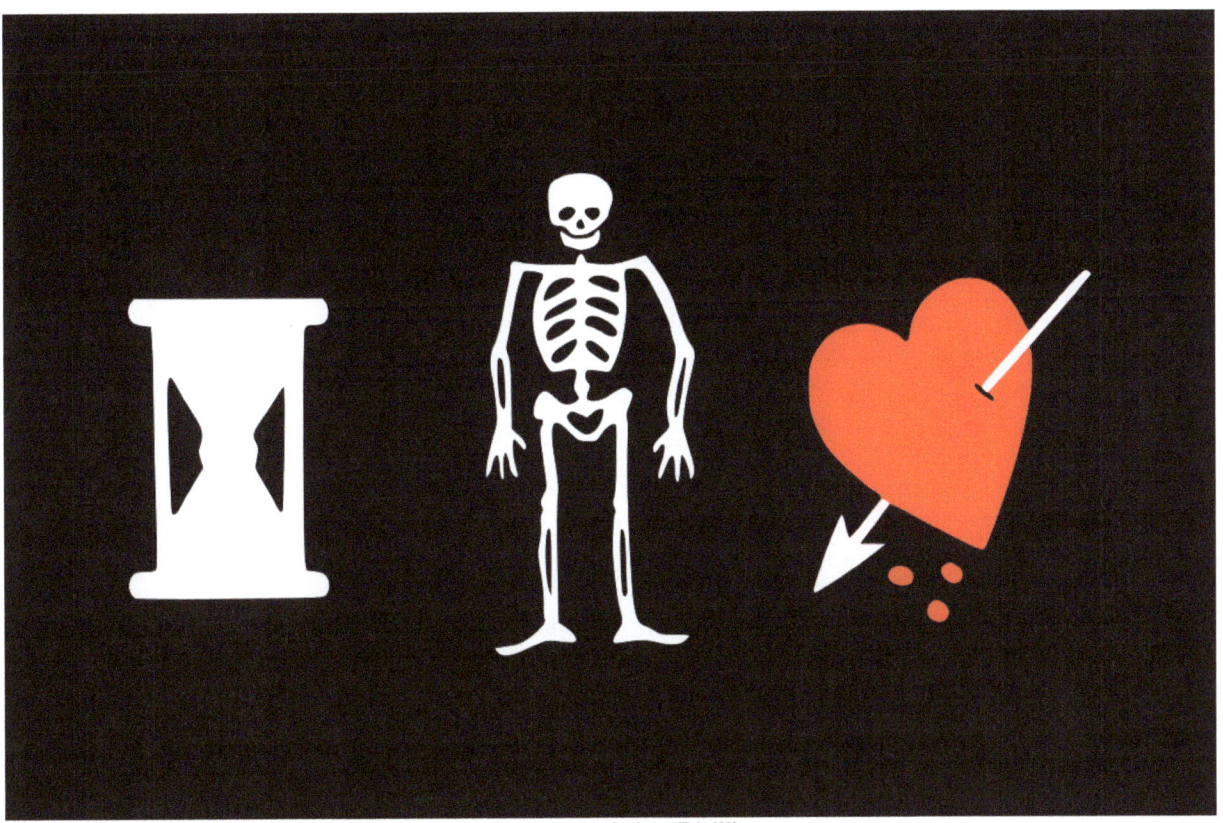

The flag of John Phillips

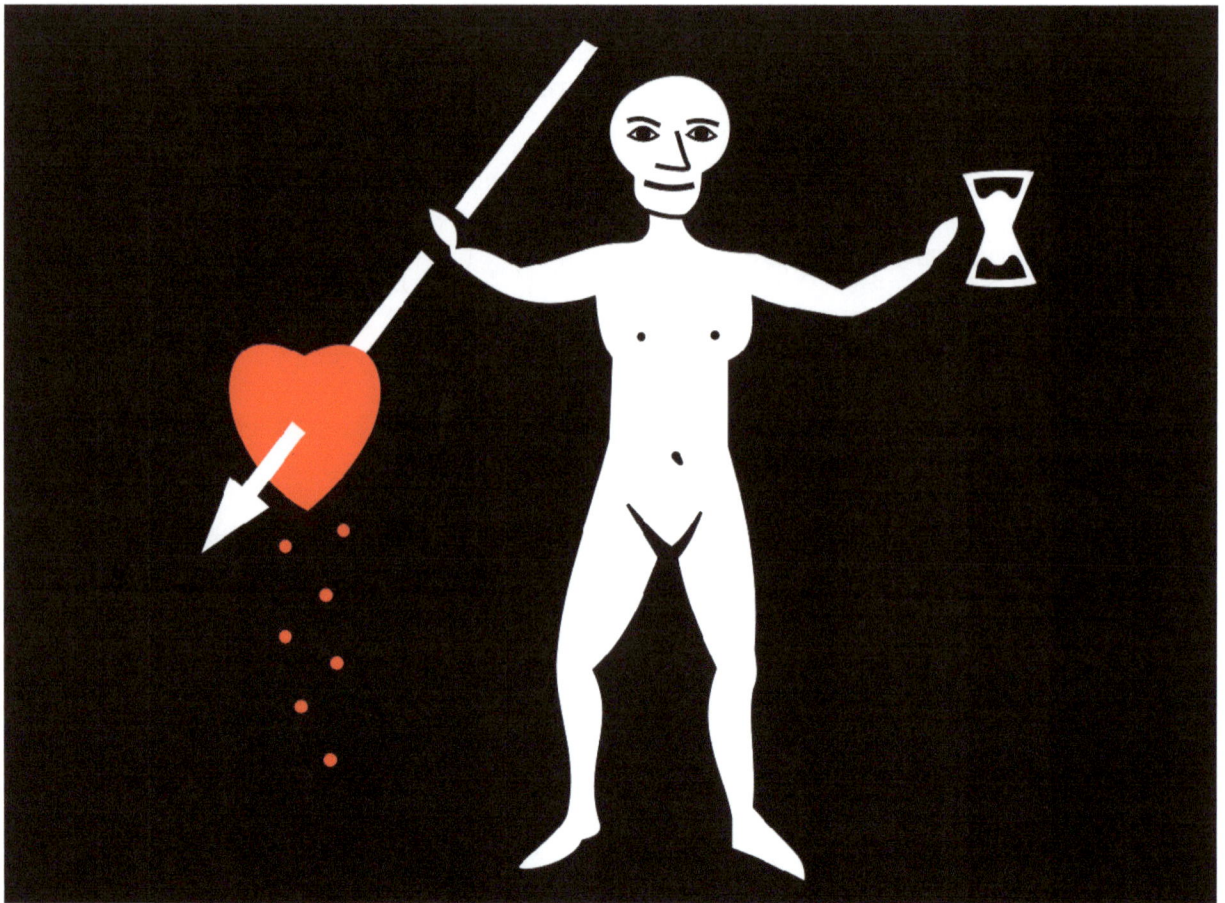

The flag of John Phillips

The two flags associated with John Phillips both have iconic elements of the Old Roger. Including the speared heart and the hourglass, one version shows Old Roger in skeletal form with the heart and the hourglass separated, whereas the other is closer to the traditional design with the Old Roger in more bodily or demonic form holding both the hourglass and the spear piercing the heart.

John Phillips was originally from Bristol and was a ship's carpenter by trade. He was on his way from England to Newfoundland when his ship was captured on 19th April 1721 by Thomas Anstis, where he was forced to join their crew as a carpenter.

In April 1722 Anstis sent Phillips and others ashore on Tobago to careen a captured ship. A British warship soon arrived which forced Anstis to abandon Phillips and flee to avoid capture. Phillips avoided capture by hiding in the woods, and later returned to Bristol with other abandoned shipmates.

Some of Phillips' fellow pirates were arrested and imprisoned soon after they arrived back in Bristol. Phillips set sail again for Newfoundland where he decided to steal a ship and return to piracy.

O 29th August 1723 with four companions, they seized a ship belonging to William Minott and named her *Revenge*. They soon agreed on their own pirate code or articles of agreement, then set sail for the West Indies, hunting ships near Barbados.

After three months without capturing any ships, their supplies ran low. Finally they found some French and English vessels. They went on to Tobago where he careened his ship.

Phillips and his crew found greater success heading north to Nova Scotia raiding New England fishing vessels between Cape Sable and Sable Island. Some 13 ships were robbed in only a few days. One of the vessels they spared belonged to William Minott, the original owner of their ship *Revenge*.

One of the prisoners captured was Andrew Harradine who conspired with other prisoners who had been forced to join the crew, and on 18th April 1724 they mutinied and killed John Phillips.

The death of John Phillips marks the end of a line of pirates who were captured by other pirates and mentored before taking to piracy on their own.

Christopher Winter > Edward England > Howell Davis > Bartholomew Roberts > John Phillips

The pirate code or articles of agreement written and signed by John Phillips and his crew is one of the few that survive from the Golden Age of Piracy.

Olivier 'La Buse' Levasseur

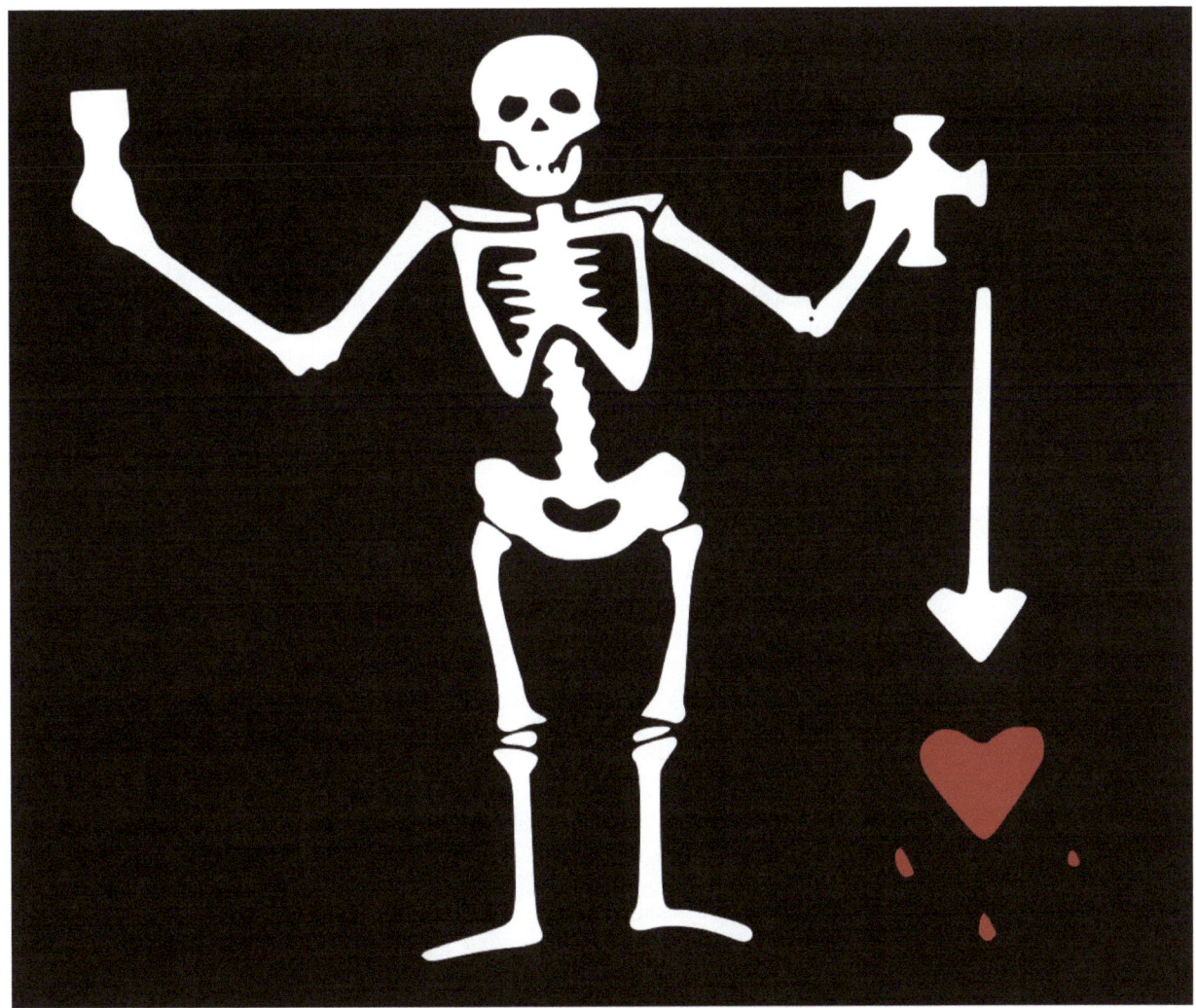

The flag of Olivier 'La Buse' Levasseur

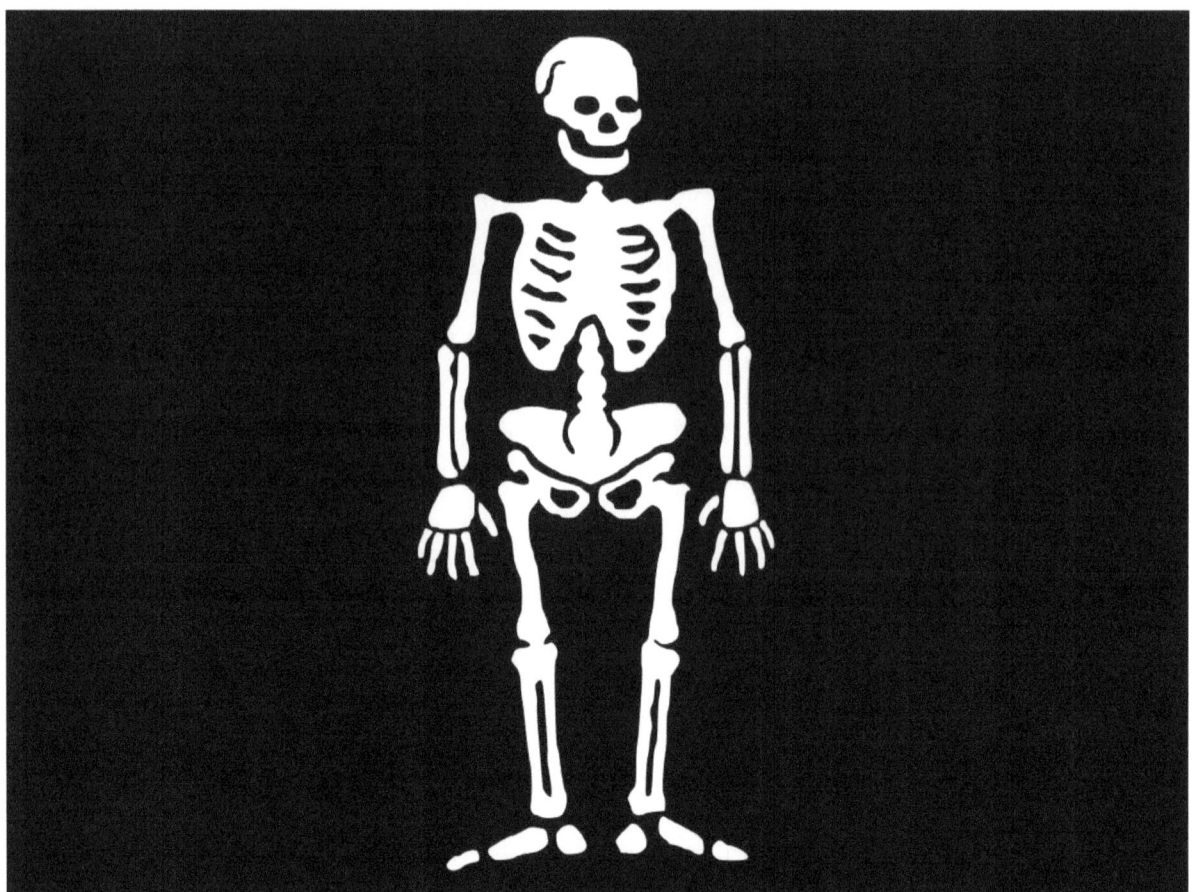
The flag of Olivier 'La Buse' Levasseur

The flag of Olivier 'La Buse' Levasseur

Olivier Levasseur was born around 1689 in Calais during the Nine Years' War (1688-1697) was nicknamed 'La Buse' (The Buzzard) because of the speed and ruthlessness with which he attacked his enemies, and also because of his ability to verbally attack his opponents, for which he also gained the nickname 'La Bouche' (The Mouth).

He is also known for allegedly hiding one of the biggest treasures in pirate history, and for leaving a cryptogram behind with clues as to the whereabouts of his treasure.

Levasseur was born into a wealthy family and received a good education before becoming a naval officer and receiving a lettre of marque from King Louis XIV.

When the War of Spanish Succession ended he was ordered to return with his ship, but instead he sailed with Benjamin Hornigold where he proved himself a good leader and a shipmate.

After a year of successful looting the Hornigold party split. Levasseur sailed with Samuel Bellamy before setting out on his own to the West African coast. His ship was lost in a storm off the coast of southern Brazil. He appeared in the Caribbean again in June 1718. He was made captain when William Moody was voted out by his crew.

He operated with Howell Davis and Thomas Cocklyn. In 1720 they attacked the port of Ouidah in what is now Benin and reduced it to ruins. Later that year he was shipwrecked in the Mozambique Channel.

From 1720 onwards Levasseur launched attacks from Île Sainte-Marie, Madagascar with John Taylor, Jasper Seagar, and Edward England.

They took part in one of the most significant acts of piracy, the capture of the Portuguese galleon *Nossa Senhora do Cabo* (Our Lady of the Cape) which was loaded full of treasures belonging to the Bishop of Goa and the Viceroy of Portugal who were both returning from India to Lisbon.

The pirates were able to board the ship without firing a single shot, as she had been damaged in a storm after which all 72 cannon were dumped overboard to prevent her from capsizing.

The haul included bars of gold and silver, golden guineas, diamonds, pearls, silk, works of art, and religious artefacts.

Levasseur had the opportunity to take advantage of an amnesty which had been offered to all pirates in the Indian Ocean, but was deterred by the fact that the French government wanted a large part of the stolen loot.

He settled o the Seychelles and attempted to live out his days anonymously and in secret, but was captured near Fort Dauphin, Madagascar and was taken to Saint-Denis, Réunion and hanged for piracy on the 7th July 1730.

Richard Worley

The flag of Richard Worley

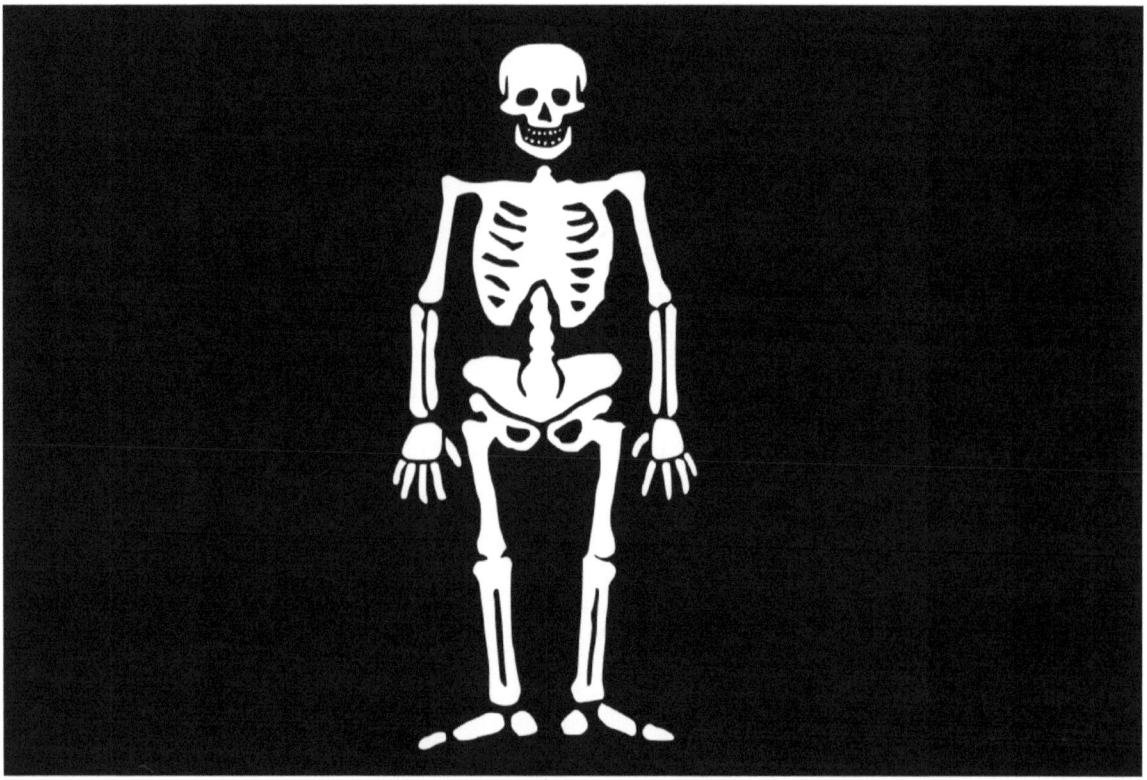
The flag of Richard Worley

There are two flags associated with Richard Worley, the first is a variation of the Skull & Crossbones in which the crossed bones are behind the skull, and the second is a skeleton which may be either an Old Roger or a representation of death or the Grim Reaper in the Danse Macabre sense, but without the addition of an hourglass or a pierced heart it is not a hundred percent certain.

Richard Worley was active in the Caribbean Sea and the east coast of the American Colonies until around 1718-1719.

His first raid along the Delaware river was mistakenly attributed to Edward Teach as he had raided the same area earlier in the year.

The haul was not riches but household goods, and as it did not take place in international waters, it was technically burglary rather than piracy.

Their second prize was more successful as they captured a ship bound for Philadelphia, and Worley gained another four crew members, and after that they seized a ship bound for Hull which was well provisioned, something that they had desperate need of as they had been running low on supplies.

They left the Delaware river and set out to the Bahamas at a time when news was spreading about the pardon being offered King George I.

The warship HMS *Phoenix* was sent out after Worley but he and his crew managed to evade capture.

While sailing around the Spanish Main he adopted his black flag with the Skull & Crossbones and agreed on a pirate code with his crew that vowed to fight to the death rather than surrender.

Worley's ship *New York's Revenge* was sailing alongside a second larger ship under captain John Cole called *New York Revenge's Revenge*.

The Governor of South Carolina Robert Johnson sent four ships after Worley and Cole. The pirate hunters split up and chased them separately.

There are different accounts of what happened next. Some say that the resulting battle occurred outside Jamestown, Virginia. Some say that the battle took place at Charles Town, South Carolina.

Either way, Worley's crew were said to be outnumbered three to one and fought a bloody last stand where all were killed except Worley and one other, who were badly wounded, brought to shore in irons, and hanged the next day on 17th Feb 1719 in a very public hanging.

Another eyewitness account says that the Governor's four ships drew up alongside, and pummelled Worley's ship with broadsides, and most of them men aboard went below deck, but Worley and a few others were killed in the cross-fire on deck.

Samuel 'Black Sam' Bellamy

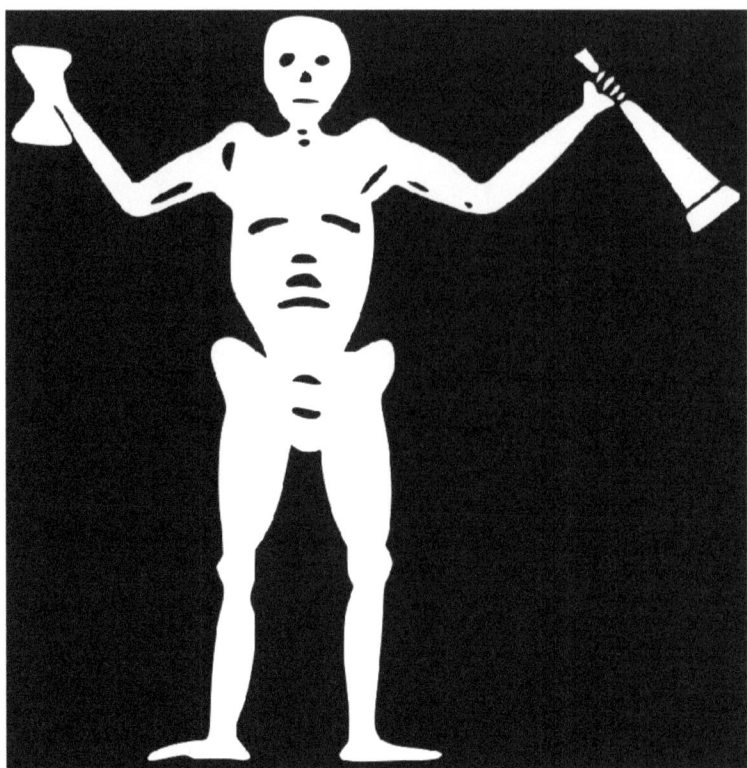

The flag of Samuel 'Black Sam' Bellamy

The flag of Samuel 'Black Sam' Bellamy

The two flags associated with Samuel Bellamy are firstly an Old Roger holding an hourglass and a trumpet (a trumpet was also used on Edward Low's green trumpeter flag), and secondly a Skull & Crossbones.

Samuel Bellamy was born around 1689 and began sailing for the Royal Navy as a teenager. In 1715 he travelled to Cape Cod, Massachusetts allegedly to seek some of his relatives there.

He left Cape Cod in early 1716 with a group of treasure hunters heading for Florida to locate a sunken Spanish treasure fleet.

His expedition was funded by the wealthy jeweller Palgraves Williams, son of Rhode Island Attorney General John Williams. The expedition was unsuccessful and they soon turned to piracy.

From Florida he made his way to the Bahamas sailing with Benjamin Hornigold and his second-in-command Edward Teach on the ship *Marianne*.

In the summer of 1716 the crew became increasingly irritated with Hornigold's refusal to attack ships from England, his home country.

By majority vote of the crew, Hornigold was removed as captain and left the vessel with his loyal followers including Edward Teach. The remaining crew of around 90 men elected Bellamy as captain of the Marianne.

Bellamy seized a vessel named *Sultana* and converted it into a galley, and with the permission of the crew gave command of the *Marianne* to his friend Palgraves Williams.

In the early spring of 1717 Bellamy captured a ship called *Wydah Gally* sailing through the Windward Passage between Hispaniola and Cuba.

It was built in 1715 and was state-of-the-art with 18 cannons, and capable of speeds of up to 13 knots (24kmph / 15mph). Bellamy chased the ship for three days before pulling up alongside and firing a single shot, at which Captain Lawrence Prince surrendered by lowering its flag.

Bellamy, true to his reputation as something of a 'Robin Hood of the seas', Prince was rewarded for his lack of resistance by being given the *Sultana* in exchange for the *Wydah*.

He removed the captain's quarters and upgraded it to hold 28 guns. Once the ship had been refitted, Bellamy turned his new flagship north along the eastern coast of the Carolinas and on to New England.

There was also a pirate captain called Charles Bellamy whose activities have been conflated with those of Samuel Bellamy, since both have been referred to as 'Captain Bellamy'.

Two months later around Cape Cod, the ship was caught in a cyclone which took Bellamy and most of his crew down with it.

The remains of the Wydah Gally were discovered in 1984, making it the first authenticated pirate vessel every to be discovered in North America.

Stede Bonnet

The flag of Stede Bonnet

The flag associated with Stede Bonnet is a loose variation of the Skull & Crossbones, but with one bone instead of two crossed, and also a heart and a stylised dagger either side.

Stede Bonnet was born in 1688 in Bridgetown Barbados to a wealthy family with an estate of over 400 acres. His father died in 1694 and Stede inherited the estate.

It is not known where he received his education but many who knew him described him as bookish, devoted to reading and study.

Bonnet married in 1709 and had three sons and a daughter. One of his sons died some time before 1715, which must have been a very traumatic event in his life.

What made him give up his lifestyle and turn to piracy is unclear. Some say that he was unhappy with married life, and perhaps unhappy with the pressures that came with running a 400 acre estate.

He had some military experience and had held the rank of major in the Barbados militia, perhaps on account of his family's wealth and land holdings. His militia service coincided with the War of Spanish Succession, but there is no record of him taking part in the fighting.

In the spring of 1717, despite having no knowledge of life at sea, he decided to become a pirate, and he contracted and local shipyard to build him a sixty ton ship, which he fitted out with ten cannons, and named it *Revenge*.

He enlisted a crew of more than seventy men, relying on his quartermaster and officer for their knowledge of sailing, and as result he was not highly respected by his crew.

Under cover of darkness, Bonnet and his crew sailed out of Carlisle Bay, Barbados and headed to the Colony of Virginia near Chesapeake Bay where they captured and plundered four vessels.

On their way to Nassau in the Bahamas, Bonnet and his crew fought a Spanish warship which they managed to escape from, but with half the crew killed or wounded, and Bonnet being seriously wounded himself. At Nassau Bonnet replaced his casualties and refitted *Revenge* with another two cannons.

While at Nassau, Bonnet met Captain Benjamin Hornigold and Edward 'Blackbeard' Teach for the first time, and still suffering from his wounds, Bonnet temporarily gave command of the *Revenge* to Blackbeard, but he remained aboard as a guest.

By December they had parted company. Bonnet sailed to the Western Caribbean, and in March 1718 they encountered a ship named *Protestant Caesar* near Honduras. The ship escaped them, and Bonnet's crew became frustrated, restless, and resistant to his command.

When Bonnet encountered Blackbeard again, Bonnet's crew deserted him and joined Blackbeard instead. Blackbeard put one of his crew Richards in charge of Bonnet's ship *Revenge* and Bonnet found himself as a guest on Blackbeard's ship *Queen Anne's Revenge*. He must have felt a sense of betrayal, but he was in no fit state to do anything about it.

Meanwhile, the ship *Revenge* under the command of Captain Richards captured a Jamaican ship, the *Adventure* captained by David Herriot. Herriot joined the pirates and now Blackbeard had three ships.

They sailed to South Carolina and blockaded the port of Charles Town. Needing a place to rest and refit their vessels, they headed north to Topsail Island, where *Queen Anne's Revenge* ran aground and was lost.

Blackbeard and Bonnet went ashore and journeyed to Bath, which was then the capital of North Carolina. Once there, both men accepted pardons from Governor Charles Eden as part of King George I's Act of Grace, assuming of course that they would renounce and give up piracy for good.

Blackbeard returned to Topsail Island while Bonnet stayed in Bath in order to get clearance to take *Revenge* to the Danish colony of St Thomas, where he intended to obtain a letter of marque and go privateering against Spanish shipping, which was granted.

He then returned to Topsail Island to find that Blackbeard had left most of their crew on the beach, robbed the *Revenge* and the other to vessels of most of their supplies, and sailed away to an unknown location on the ship *Adventure* with all of the loot.

Bonnet resumed command of *Revenge* taking the crew that Blackbeard had abandoned, and soon after he received news that Blackbeard was moored in Ocracoke Inlet, North Carolina. He set sail and attempted to track down Blackbeard but could not find him. He would never see him again.

Although he ever gave up hope of reaching St Thomas and obtaining his letter of marque, they badly needed supplies, and St Thomas was in the middle of hurricane season.

In a bid to preserve his pardon, Bonnet adopted the pseudonym of Captain Thomas and renamed *Revenge* to *Royal James*, but by July 1718 he had returned to full piracy, capturing two ships in Delaware Bay *Francis* and *Fortune*.

They arrived in the estuary of Cape Fear River to refit and repair the *Royal James* which was leaking badly. They stayed there another 45 days hoping to wait out the hurricane season there.

News had reached Charles Town that they were moored in the Cape Fear River. Governor of South Carolina Robert Johnson authorised Colonel William Rhett to lead a naval expedition against the pirates. Rhett arrived at the mouth of Cape Fear on 26th September 1718 with two ships and a hundred and thirty militia men.

The Battle of Cape Fear River lasted over six hours, with several ships running around and becoming immobile. The rising of the tide tipped the balance in favour of Rhett and his crew and he arrested the pirates and returned to Charles Town on 3rd October with his prisoners.

On the 24th October Bonnet and Herriot escaped and with two others headed for the north shore of Charles Town Harbour. Governor Johnson put a £700 bounty was put on their heads, and sent out search teams to recapture them.

The others were shot, and only Bonnet remained. He surrendered and was tried on 10th November 1718. He was hanged at White Point Garden on 10th December 1718.

Thomas Nichols

The flag of Thomas Nichols

The flag of Thomas Nichols

The flag of Thomas Nichols

The flags associated with Thomas Nichols include a pierced heart and a Skull & Crossbones which is also the flag of The Flying Gang, a group of pirates of which Nichols was a member, operating out of New Providence Island in The Bahamas.

Little is known of Thomas Nichols' life or career outside of The Flying Gang. Other members included Benjamin Hornigold, Henry Jennings, Edward Teach, Charles Vane, Jack Rackham, Stede Bonnet, Francis Leslie, and Josiah Burgess.

In 1703 and again in 1706 a combined force of French and Spanish ships attacked Nassau. Many of the settlers left the island and it was abandoned by any representatives of the English government. Nassau was then taken over by English privateers who used it as a base to attack French and Spanish ships. It became a busy port where privateers could repair, refit, and resupply, much the same as they had back in Port Royal before Henry Morgan had banned them from doing so.

By 1713 the War of Spanish Succession was over, but many British privateers were slow to receive the news, or had become addicted to the lifestyle and chose to ignore the news, carrying on raiding all and any ships they could regardless of their country of origin or state of relations with their own country of origin. This marks their transition from privateers to pirates.

Word and reputation spread, and more and more unemployed privateers arrived in Nassau looking for a crew to join, swelling their ranks to such a degree that their fleet of ships could take on the Royal Navy. They achieved wealth and fame by raiding salvagers attempting to recover gold from the sunken Spanish treasure fleet.

The two dominant pirates of The Flying Gang were Benjamin Hornigold and Henry Jennings, who were fierce rivals, both of whom had mentored a series of pirates who went on to be successful in their own right. Despite their fierce rivalry, they nevertheless worked together to protect the pirates' way of life on Nassau.

Benjamin Hornigold had accepted the pardon of King George delivered by Governor Woodes Rogers in 1718, and was then commissioned to hunt down the remaining pirates. While Charles Vane and Edward Teach evaded capture for the time being, Hornigold caught 10 pirates, 9 of which were executed in December 1718.

The British had regained control of Nassau, The Republic of Pirates had fallen, and the Flying Gang had disbanded, many continuing their activities elsewhere in the Caribbean and the east coast of North America.

Walter Kennedy

The flag of Walter Kennedy

The flag of Walter Kennedy

There are two flags associated with Walter Kennedy. The first is very similar to that of Jean Thomas Dulaien and is a combination of the Skull & Crossbones (or a severed head with crossbones) and an Old Roger. The second flag features a Skull & Crossbones on the left with the bones behind the skull in a similar style to Emanuel Wynn and Richard Worley, with a depiction of Walter Kennedy himself holding a sword in the middle, and then an hourglass on the right hand side.

Walter Kennedy was born around 1695 in Wapping, East London where he was a burglar and a pickpocket for a time before becoming an apprentice to his father who was a smith. When his father died he decided to join the Royal Navy during the War of Spanish Succession. During this time it is probable that he heard tales of the exploits of famous pirates like Henry Morgan and Henry Every, and he likely became attracted to the idea of becoming a pirate himself.

He sailed with Woodes Rogers' fleet to the Bahamas in 1718 in a ship called *Buck*. *Buck* was then sent to Havana to reassure the Spanish governor that they were there to capture pirates. On the way to Havana however, the crew, including some recently pardoned pirates, mutinied, and killed the captain and other crew members who did not join the mutiny.

Among the mutineers was Howell Davis who was elected captain. While on sire on the island of Principe they were ambushed by the Portuguese, and Kennedy was the only one of the to make it back to their ship alive. Bartholomew Roberts was then elected as captain and they sailed to Surinam in the hope of capturing a ship.

Kennedy was left in charge of Roberts' ship the *Royal Rover* and a large part of his crew. He abandoned Roberts and declared himself captain. The crew decided to give up piracy and sail back to Ireland. Although Kennedy had served briefly in the Royal Navy before turning to piracy, he lacked training and knowledge in navigation, which was the responsibility of deck officers.

The crew were furious that he had taken over as captain without the required skills, and they nearly threw him overboard but decided against it on account of his courage.

Due to poor navigation, instead of Ireland they arrived on the north-west cost of Scotland and tried to pass themselves off as mere shipwrecked sailors rather than pirates, but instead of blending in and not attracting attention, their unruly drunken behaviour gave them away, seventeen were arrested in Edinburgh and put on trial for acts of piracy, and nine of them were hanged.

Kennedy managed to avoid arrest in Edinburgh and made it to Dublin where he quickly spent all of his loot. He returned to Deptford in London and being accused of theft he ended up in Bridewell prison. One of the inmates there had been a mate on a ship that Kennedy had taken. He recognised Kennedy immediately and denounced him as a pirate. Kennedy was then moved to Marshalsea prison and tried for acts of piracy. He was hanged at Execution Dock on 21st July 1721.

5. The Later Years

By the 1720s the world had lost patience with the pirates. Piracy was playing havoc with trade and the economy, and efforts were increased to suppress it. Nations vowed to deal with the pirates once and for all, and in such a way that would make an example of them, to deter anyone else from following these outlaws of the sea in their lifestyle choices. By 1729 over 300 pirates had been hanged in London, the American Colonies, the Caribbean, and the Gold Coast of West Africa.

The nations affected by piracy increased their navies and their capability to protect ships and to hunt down pirates. These pirates must have sensed that their way of life was coming to an end, that they were hunted men, and that their days were numbered. The hunters had become the hunted. The number of options still open to them was dwindling. After the deadline of the 5th September 1718 had passed, so too had any hope of a pardon. Many of those who had accepted it, had returned to piracy shortly afterwards. Some attempted to disappear into thin air, some tried their luck in Africa, and some allegedly buried their treasure in secret locations.

As news of their capture, trial, and execution emerged with greater frequency in the media of the day, such as the *London Gazette* and the *Daily Post*, the detailed accounts and testimonies from these trials must have at first brought about in the public a sense of shock, horror, disapproval of their actions, and a fear of the threat these pirates posed, but also a sense of relief that something was being done about the menace that they inflicted on the seas, which gave way to a curiosity about what drove them to do what they did.

Even as the Golden Age of Piracy was coming to an end, the first book on the subject, *A General History of the Pyrates*, was published in 1724 under the pseudonym Captain Charles Johnson, which is believed to be a pen name of Daniel Defoe. Defoe was fascinated by pirates, travel, trade, crime, colonisation, etc. and he was a friend of Woodes Rogers who could well have provided Defoe with a series of accounts of the activities of the pirates based on his time as Governor of The Bahamas and his attempt to suppress them.

The book was a success because it capitalised on the public thirst for information about the phenomenon of piracy, some of which they had heard about in the news, and some by hearsay and rumour. Some of the content of the book is variously described by scholars as being a matter of invention, dramatic or artistic license, and moral tales. Some of this is perhaps borne out of the fascination that the author had for the subject. Over time, the accounts in this book, and others like it elevated these infamous and notorious pirates to an almost mythical status.

While the Golden Age of Piracy had effectively ended, piracy itself did not end. Despite the clamping down on piracy by world powers, there were still some from time to time who weighed up the ever increasing risks and still decided to take their chances, motivated by desperation, disillusionment, anger, fear, escape, thirst for power, illegal trade, revenge or any number of circumstances.

The flag designs that pirates continued to use to identify themselves were informed by and built upon an established tradition of signs and symbols. While other icons and elements were incorporated into the design of a pirate flag over the next few hundred years, the skull or death's head was still a popular and effective icon.

Anonymous

An anonymous flag

This flag design is based on the description given by a William Falconer in 1783. A black flag, with a 'death's head', an hourglass, and also unusually, a battle-axe. No mention of the pirate or pirates who used this flag is known.

Ching Shih

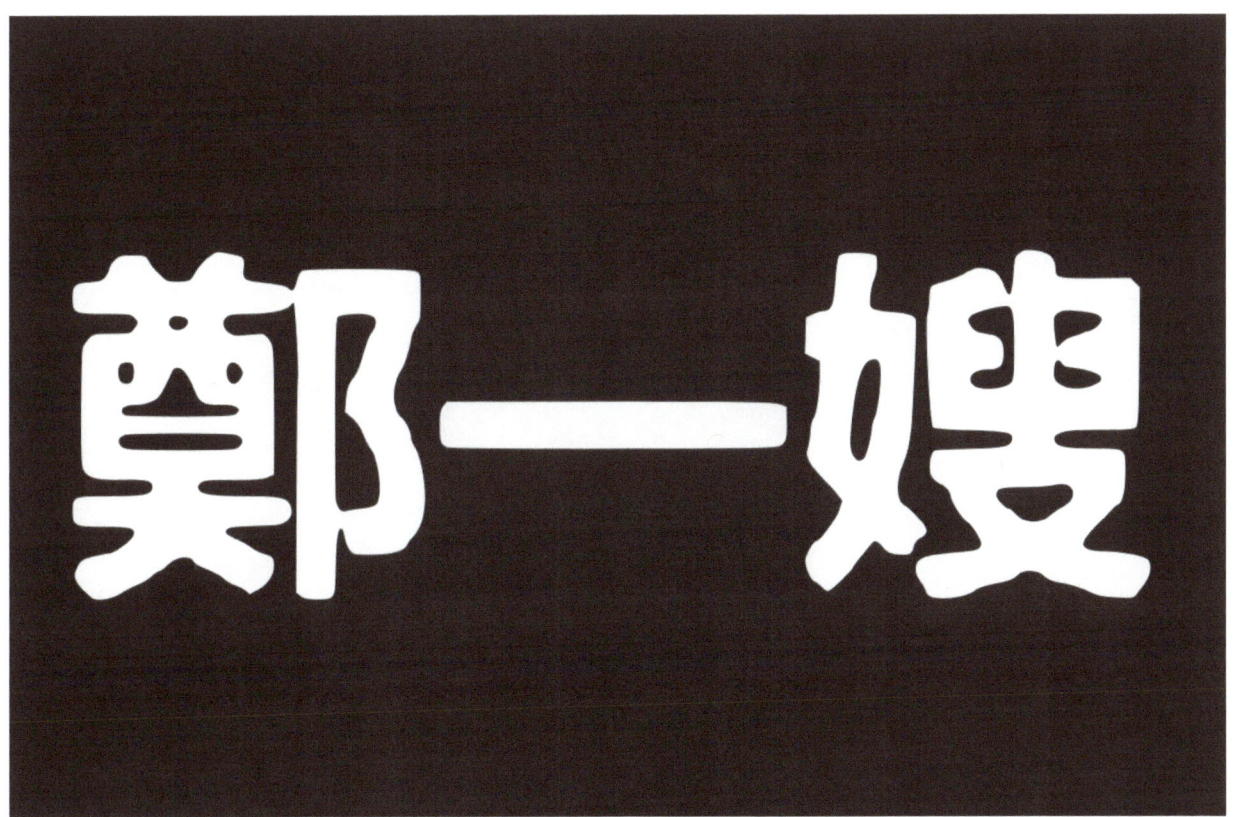
The flag of Ching Shih

The flag of Ching Shih

The flag of Ching Shih

The first flag associated with Ching Shih has a black background with Chinese calligraphy in white:

鄭一嫂

This can be transliterated and translated as follows:

Cheng I Sao
Wife of Cheng I

Cheung Yi Sao
Wife of Cheung Yi

Zheng Yisao
Wife of Zheng Yi

The second flag is the flag of the Red Flag Fleet which shows a Chinese ship or junk on a red background.

The last flag associated with Ching Shih shows a red background with a variation of the Skull & Crossbones, but with crossed swords instead of crossed bones, similar to the crossed swords of Jack Rackham and Edward England, but with one of the swords emerging through the ocular cavity (eye socket) of the skull.

Ching Shih was born Shih Yang in 1775 in Guangdong province. She worked in a floating brothel in Guangzhou where she met Cheng I, a notorious pirate whom she married in 1801. She participated in his acts of piracy and was granted 50% control and share of the operations.

Cheng I formed a coalition unifying former rival pirate gangs into what became known as the Red Flag Fleet. Their power and control of criminality increased and their sphere of influence expanded, and by 1804 they had become unstoppable.

Cheng I died in 1807 in Vietnam while his ship was caught in a typhoon. Ching Shih asserted control and won the approval and support of Cheng's family. She gained the trust and loyalty of her lieutenants by sharing her power with them. She was a master tactician and was able to solidify partnerships that would secure her position against any potential rivals.

By 1810 she commanded over 1,800 vessels and over 70,000 men, women, and children, pirates, a network of spies in the Qing Dynasty, and a network of farmers to supply the fleet.

Because she controlled the entire criminal element in the South China Sea, she was able to grant safe passage to merchants travelling through who were willing to pay a fee. If they did not pay a fee however, then there was no guarantee that their ships and goods would not be plundered, and of course, they were.

Such a rise to power and aggressive control over such a wide area had to be kept under control, and in order to achieve this, Ching Shih introduced a strict code.

- If you disobey an order, you get your head chopped off and your body thrown in the ocean.
- If you steal anything from the common plunder before it has been divided up, you get your head chopped off and your body thrown in the ocean.
- If you rape anyone without permission from the leader of your squadron, you get your head chopped off and your body thrown in the ocean.
- If you have consensual sex with anyone while on duty, you get your head chopped off and your body thrown in the ocean, and the woman involved would have something heavy tied to her and thrown in the ocean.
- If you loot a town or ship of anything at all or otherwise harass them when they have paid tribute, you get your head chopped off and your body thrown into the ocean.
- If you take shore-leave without permission, you get your head chopped off and body thrown into the ocean.
- If you try to leave the organisation, you get your ears chopped off.
- Captured women who were not considered pretty were to be set free unharmed. Captured women who were considered pretty could be divided up or purchased by members of the Red Flag Fleet. If a pirate was awarded or purchased a pretty woman, he was then considered married to her and was expected to treat her accordingly. If he didn't, he got his head chopped off and his body thrown in the ocean.

The Qing Imperial Government had repeatedly tried to destroy Ching Shih's fleet in a series of attacks, but Ching Shih was also a gifted military tactician and none of these attacks were successful. She also managed to seize and pillage the government ships.

British and Portuguese ships attacked the Red Flag Fleet in a series of battles in 1809, after which Ching Shih accepted an offer of amnesty from the Qing Imperial Government promising that all pirates who agreed to surrender and end their piracy were allowed to keep their loot,. 60 pirates would be banished, 151 would be exiled, and 126 would be put to death, and the remaining 16,900 pirates had to surrender their weapons.

Ching Shih negotiated to be able to keep 120 ships. She also arranged for Cheung Po Tsai, Ching Shih's second in command, a position as captain in the Qing Guangdong Navy.

Her marriage to Cheung Po was officially recognised despite widows being restricted from remarrying. She was also made a lady of the aristocracy by imperial decree.

After Cheung Po died at sea in 1822, Ching Shih moved to Macau with her family and opened a gambling house. She used the 120 ships she had been allowed to keep in the salt trade.

In her later years she was an advisor to Lin Zexu in battling the British during the First Opium War of 1839.

She was one of the few pirates ever to be able to retire while holding on to her treasure. She retired wealthy, ennobled, and surrounded by her family in 1844, she died aged 69.

She is arguably the most successful pirate in history.

The Florida Straits Pirates

The flag of the Florida Straits Pirates

The flag associated with the so called Florida Straits Pirates is based on an account of an attack in May 1822 on a ship called *Belvidere* from Massachusetts in the Florida Strait.

The *Belivdere* was attacked by pirates in a schooner. The attack was repelled, but the identity of the schooner or the captain was never known. On the red flag, the skull or 'death's head' is jawless, and the cross is a 'cross potent' or 'crutch cross'.

Sources

Exquemelin, Alexandre. The Buccaneers of America: A true account of the most remarkable assaults committed of late years upon the coasts of West Indies by the Buccaneers of Jamaica and Tortuga. London: T. Evans (Pantianos Classics), 1684. Reprinted 1914.

Johnson, Captain Charles. A General History of the Pyrates: From Their First Rise and Settlement in the Island Of Providence, To the Present Time. London: T. Warner (Forgotten Books, Facsimile Reprint), 1724. Reprinted 2018.

Ellms, Charles. The Pirates Own Book: Authentic Narratives of the Most Celebrated Sea Robbers. Boston (New York): Dover Publications Inc., 1837. Reprinted 1993.

Cordingly, David. Life among the Pirates: The Romance and the Reality. London: Abacus, 1995.

Cordingly, David. Spanish Gold: Captain Woodes Rogers & the Pirates of the Caribbean. London: Bloomsbury, 2011.

Wikipedia: Piracy (https://en.wikipedia.org/wiki/Piracy). Retrieved 1st August 2020.

Wikipedia: Piracy in the Caribbean (https://en.wikipedia.org/wiki/Piracy_in_the_Caribbean). Retrieved 1st August 2020.

Wikipedia: The Golden Age of Piracy (https://en.wikipedia.org/wiki/Golden_Age_of_Piracy). Retrieved 1st August 2020.

Wikipedia: Buccaneers (https://en.wikipedia.org/wiki/Buccaneer). Retrieved 1st August 2020.

Wikipedia: The Pirate Round (https://en.wikipedia.org/wiki/Pirate_Round). Retrieved 1st August 2020

www.ingramcontent.com/pod-product-compliance
Lightning Source LLC
Chambersburg PA
CBHW041113070526
44584CB00002B/149